THE
FRACTURED
KINGDOM

THE FRACTURED KINGDOM

Uniting Modern Christianity Through The Historical Jesus

JEAN-PIERRE ISBOUTS

Morehouse Publishing
NEW YORK

Morehouse Publishing, 19 East 34th Street, New York, NY 10016

Morehouse Publishing is an imprint of Church Publishing Incorporated.

Cover design by David Baldeosingh Rotstein

A record of this book is available from the Library of Congress.

ISBN 978-1-64065-643-7 (hardcover)
ISBN 978-1-64065-644-4 (ebook)

If a kingdom is divided against itself,
that kingdom cannot stand.
And if a house is divided against itself,
that house will not be able to stand.

Mark 3:24–25

CONTENTS

Today, the Christian community in America is divided along the fault lines of our nation's culture wars. What is forgotten in these debates is what Jesus himself said about how to heal a divided nation. That is the purpose of this book, in part by using the one element that binds Christians together: the Lord's Prayer, also known as the *Our Father*.

Part I
Rediscovering the Historical Jesus

The Galilee of Jesus' time, traditionally the breadbasket of the Middle East, was ruthlessly exploited by King Herod and his son Antipas in order to fund the construction of cities such as Sebaste, Caesarea, Sepphoris, and Tiberias. This produced a vast crisis with thousands of dispossessed rural families. It is likely that this crisis informed and shaped Jesus' ministry.

The Gospels do not tell us about the years of Jesus' adolescence. This chapter speculates that Jesus and his father, Joseph, who were both *tektoi* or "skilled workers" as Mark tells us, must have been conscripted for the construction of the new capital of Sepphoris, just a few miles from Nazareth. Jesus may have been introduced to the large Pharisaic community in this new city, who possibly tutored him in Scripture.

The sojourn in the camp of a leading dissident, John the Baptist, was a cathartic experience for the young rabbi Jesus. Here was a charismatic speaker who seemed to have a solution for the ills of the time. This was the coming of the Messiah who would "cleanse" the nation of the godless Romans and return the land to an obedient kingdom ruled by God.

Jesus formulated a new vision for the age-old Jewish dream of the Kingdom of God: a new basis for a compassionate society, not as a result of regime change, but as a grassroots movement of people power. He summarized the key tenets of his ministry in a prayer he taught his disciples.

Part II
The Lord's Prayer: A Blueprint for Unity

Jesus' idea of referring to God as *Abba* or *Abwoon* in Aramaic (meaning "Papa" or "Daddy") was a radical innovation. Jesus tried to eliminate the great distance that existed between God and human beings in ancient Judaism and offer a more direct form of spirituality.

These words are not an appeal for liberation in a political sense but rather, a petition: an article of faith. To be a disciple of Jesus, one must believe in the possibility of the Kingdom of God as a society based on faith, love, and social justice. It means we should heal our communities, rather than sowing division.

Bread made from wheat was the principal staple in Jesus' time, as it is today. But the story of the miraculous multiplication refers to loaves made from barley. Barley was grown as feed for farm animals. In other words, the story tells us that the crisis in Galilee had reduced people to eating animal fodder. There is an obvious parallel to our modern times.

Matthew refers to *debts*, but Luke refers to *sins*, perhaps prompted by the fact that the Aramaic word *hova* can mean both "debt" and "sin." The case for "debt" is supported by numerous references in the Gospels. But Luke interprets the verse as the need to be merciful; that if we expect God to be merciful toward us, then we have the moral duty to extend that same mercy and tolerance to others.

One view interprets the word *test* as an apocalyptic clash, a battle between good and evil that would herald the Kingdom of God at the End Times. But for Jesus, the Kingdom was a matter of the heart: a perfect state of faith and goodwill toward one another.

There is no question that we are surrounded by evil in our world, just as in Jesus' day. Our modern society is inherently a competitive one, in which greed and selfishness are often allowed to flourish unchecked. What Jesus is talking about is the very opposite of evil: *agápē*, the selfless love that is at the core of his teachings.

For many Christians, Jesus' crucifixion and resurrection are the two defining elements of Christianity. In this reconstruction, based on historical data, we examine the charges that led to Jesus' arrest and indictment by the high priest Caiaphas, and the question of who bears responsibility for his murder.

Even before Christianity became an officially tolerated religion in the late third century, different Christian currents emerged about the purpose of Jesus' teachings and the nature of his divinity. But we must not allow ourselves to be waylaid by disparate doctrinal concerns. We must come together as a community of Christians, using the Kingdom vision as our principal foundation.

GLOSSARY

Archelaus, Herod — Son of King Herod who became the *ethnarch* ("ruler of the people") of Judea and Samaria after Herod's death.

Antipas, Herod — Son of King Herod who became the *tetrarch* ("ruler of a fourth") of Galilee and Perea after Herod's death.

BCE — "Before the Common Era," a term used by scholars to denote the period previously referred to as "BC" or "Before Christ."

CE — The "Common Era," a term used by scholars to denote the period previously referred to as "AD" or "Anno Domini."

Caiaphas — Son-in-law of the high priest Anas, who served as high priest from ca. 18 CE to 36 CE and who presided over the indictment of Jesus.

Essenes — A group who formed a "commune" of sorts to pursue an ascetic lifestyle entirely based on the Torah, the Law.

Herod the Great — Idumean nobleman who served as Rome's vassal king of Roman Palestine from 37 BCE to 4 BCE.

John

The Gospel of John, believed to have been compiled between ca. 85 and 95 CE, possibly in Asia Minor. It is traditionally credited to either the apostle "John, son of Zebedee," or the apostle John, "the disciple (whom) Jesus loved (John 19:26; 35). The Gospel itself makes no claim about its authorship, but it does state that its account is based on the testimony of the apostle John, "the beloved disciple," and adds in its final paragraphs that "this is the disciple who is testifying to these things and has written them, and we know that his testimony is true" (John 21:24).

Josephus

First-century Jewish historian who was captured during the First Jewish War of 66–70 CE but who subsequently moved to Rome under the patronage of Emperor Vespasian. His book *Antiquities of the Jews* is a major source about the social and political conditions of first-century Roman Palestine.

Luke

The Gospel of Luke, believed to have been compiled between ca. 75 and 85 CE, partly based on the Gospel of Mark as well as Q. The author is traditionally associated with the person who traveled with Paul on his journey to Greece and accompanied him on his last and fateful voyage to Jerusalem. His Greek is heavily influenced by the "biblical" style of the Septuagint, the Greek translation of the Hebrew Scriptures composed in Alexandria, Egypt.

This would suggest that this author wrote for a Diaspora Judeo-Christian community somewhere in the Mediterranean region. The author of Luke is also traditionally credited with writing the book of the Acts of the Apostles.

Mark

The Gospel of Mark, believed to have been compiled in Rome in the years during the First Jewish War of 66–70 CE. It is the oldest Gospel in the New Testament. The author is traditionally identified with (John) Mark, the friend of Paul who visited the community at Colossae (Colossians 4:10) and is also mentioned in the closing greetings of Peter's letter from Rome. But the actual text of the Gospel does not mention a Mark, nor does it identify its author.

Matthew

The Gospel of Matthew, believed to have been compiled between ca. 75 and 85 CE, partly based on the Gospel of Mark as well as the Q sayings document. In fact, Bishop Papias of Hieropolis (Asia Minor) wrote in the early second century CE that the author of Matthew had compiled a collection of sayings by Jesus, written in Hebrew. The author is traditionally identified as the tax collector named Levi whom Jesus found in the customs house in Capernaum and subsequently joined him as an apostle (Matthew 9:9). However, the Matthew Gospel is written in an erudite and elegant Greek that bespeaks the hand of an

	educated scribe, not a Galilean tax collector in a small township like Capernaum.
Messiah (*Mashiach*)	A Jewish redeemer who would liberate his people from foreign occupation and establish a kingdom of God. In the Gospels, the term is translated as *Christos* or "Christ."
Mikveh (plural *mikva'ot*)	Bath, used by observant Jews for ritual immersion.
Mishnah	The first written collection of Jewish oral traditions, featuring debates among rabbinic sages about the application of the Torah. Many scholars accept that the Pharisaic debates, known as the "Oral Law," form the basis of the Mishnah, which was compiled by Judah ha-Nasi in the third century.
Palestine (*Palaistínē*)	The Greek name for the territory of ancient Israel as used by Herodotus et al., based on the Assyrian term "Palashtu."
Passover	Major Jewish festival that celebrates the deliverance of the Israelites from slavery in Egypt, as described in the Book of Exodus. Jesus is believed to have been arrested on the eve of Passover of 30 or 33 CE.
Pharisees	A group composed of both priests and pious laymen who were passionately devoted to the application of the Jewish Law in everyday life, including its rules of ritual purity.

Philip, Herod	Son of King Herod who became the *tetrarch* ("ruler of a fourth") of the Gaulanitis after Herod's death.
Pilate, Pontius	Roman prefect of Judea between 26 and 36 CE. Pilate was dismissed from his post because of excessive cruelty.
Prophets, the	The Books of the Prophets form the second division of Hebrew Scripture, known as the *Nevi'im*. Jesus refers to the two divisions of the Hebrew Bible in his time as "the law and the prophets."
Q	A putative document of mainly Jesus' sayings (after the German word *Quelle*) that scholars believe must have been circulating in the mid-first century, and which forms an important source for the Gospels of Luke and Matthew.
Qumran	An ancient settlement in the desert, close to the Dead Sea, which was responsible for hiding the Dead Sea Scrolls in nearby caves.
Sadducees	Deeply conservative, the Sadducees controlled the elaborate apparatus of ritual sacrifice at the Second Temple, including the collection of tithes from every Jew in Judea and throughout the Diaspora.
Saul (*Sha'ul*)	The name of Paul before he adopted its Latinized version, *Paulus,* prior to his first missionary journey.

Shavuot	Also known as the Feast of Reaping, the Festival of First Fruits, or Pentecost, one of the three main Jewish festivals celebrated fifty days after Passover.
Succoth	The Feast of Tabernacles, one of the three main Jewish festivals that is celebrated in the month of Tishri (September/October).
Synoptic Gospels	The Gospels of Mark, Luke and Matthew, called the "Synoptics" because of their similarity.
Thomas, Gospel of	A sayings document about Jesus commonly dated to the late first century or second century, but which may be based on an earlier source.
Torah	The first division of the Hebrew Bible, known as the Jewish Law, also known as the Pentateuch or the "Five Books of Moses."
Zealots	A group of Jews who practiced passive resistance against the Roman census of 6 CE. Many decades later, they may have developed into the militant wing that led the First Jewish War against the Romans in 66 CE.

INTRODUCTION

The narrow road was located just off Coldwater Canyon, the exclusive enclave running across the rugged Santa Monica Mountains that since the 1930s has been the destination of choice for Hollywood royalty. As the road dipped past the entrance gate and moved deeper into the crevice, the sound of traffic fell away, and we were surrounded by soaring cypresses that sheltered a beautiful home. Its multiple levels cascaded gently down the canyon.

"The house that Ben-Hur built," Charlton Heston said proudly; "it's the proceeds from that picture that allowed me to build it."

We had been invited to the home of the Academy Award–winning actor because I had written and directed two programs of *Charlton Heston's Voyage through the Bible* with him, which unexpectedly had become a commercial and critical success. What's more, Charlton—"Chuck" to his friends—found that he liked the narrative cadence of my writing.

"You write the way I speak," he said. "Not many people get that."

We had decided that we would collaborate on a book about his and his wife Lydia's years in the film industry, titled *Charlton Heston's Hollywood*. I thought it would be interesting to use Heston's career as a prism to project the history of postwar Hollywood from the 1940s to the end of the twentieth century. After all, he was the only American actor who could claim a career spanning from Cecil B. DeMille to James Cameron, two directors at the opposite poles of American cinema.

"How shall we begin?" he asked.

I explained that I had brought a video camera, which I would use to conduct a series of interviews with him over the next few weeks. My office would arrange for the tapes to be transcribed, and then I would use the material to start crafting the story.

"Sounds like a plan," he said.

As we settled down in his study and the video gear was being set up, we spent a moment talking about the movie memorabilia that decorated the walls. I had, quite literally, grown up with Heston's films—from *The Ten Commandments* to *Ben Hur*, and from *Khartoum* to *The Omega Man* and *Soylent Green*.

"That was my best performance," he said, following my gaze to a poster of *Khartoum* on the wall. "Working with Larry Olivier was a wonderful experience."

But an hour into our first interview, when I asked him what he thought was his most memorable achievement, he surprised me. "You see," he said, "the early 1960s was a very difficult time in our country. For the first time, we could see on television what was happening in the South, in real time. The Alabama police using German shepherds and water cannon to tear into peaceful Black protesters, for example. I felt I had to do something to meet the moment. So I went down to Oklahoma City, where they were planning a demonstration against some restaurants that refused to serve Black patrons."

When MGM learned of Heston's planned visit, the studio bosses were none too pleased. *Ben Hur* was still in release, and *El Cid* was in postproduction, with a scheduled premiere in just six months. But Heston was not to be dissuaded. "Come on, guys," he told the studio, *"El Cid* isn't going to be in the theaters for another six months. *Ben Hur* has been playing since 1959; everyone's seen it already anyway. Are you telling me people won't go back for a second look because I picket a couple of restaurants?" So the studio demurred, Heston went to Oklahoma City, and the protestors got what they wanted: massive publicity.

Two years later, in 1963, Heston agreed to take over as president of the Screen Actors Guild (SAG) when word reached Hollywood that Martin Luther King was planning a march on Washington, DC. King wanted Americans of every race, religion, and background to join—including stars from Hollywood. "I thought it over," Heston said, "and began to spread the word, in the hope of organizing a delegation of Hollywood actors." For some this came as a surprise, because Heston was associated with SAG's conservative wing and tended to favor Republican policy issues. In contrast, the Guild's progressive wing was headed—naturally—by Marlon Brando. "Look, Chuck," Brando said during a planning meeting at Heston's house, "we should chain ourselves to the Lincoln Memorial . . . or lie down in front of the White House and block Pennsylvania Avenue." No, said Heston, if we are going to go, we are going to do it peacefully.

And, much to his surprise, the *crème de la crème* of Hollywood actors, twenty in all, decided to join him in Washington, DC, including Burt Lancaster, Paul Newman, Jim Garner, and Sidney Poitier. Heston was deeply moved by the experience.

Here were people of all walks of life, he said: liberals and conservatives, Christian and Jews, Catholics and Protestants, Blacks and Whites, all walking arm in arm for civil rights. Heston was at the head of the march, right behind King. "It was," he said, "my finest moment."[1]

Would such a moment be possible today? Could our nation, liberals and conservatives alike, once again walk arm in arm in support of social justice and civil rights? It is perhaps no exaggeration to say that our country is more divided than at any time since the nineteenth century. According to a 2022 poll, some 62 percent of Americans, both Republicans and Democrats, believe our democracy is in jeopardy.[2] And yet, we are facing an extraordinary opportunity: to rebuild a nation that has been ravaged by a pandemic and a recession, torn by political partisanship, and deeply cleft along the fault lines of social and economic inequality.

Charlton Heston during the March on Washington.

How can we rise to the occasion? What kind of moral compass can help us to navigate the immense difficulties ahead, and heal our great divide?

To compound the problem, the Christian community in the United States and the world at large is more divided than ever. Not since the Vietnam War has American Christianity been so split between progressives and conservatives, and not since the Civil War has this divide led to such fierce acrimony, hatred, and even violence.

Some might point out that this has been the case from the very beginning, and that the Christian world has always known divisions. Even during its founding years, the traditional strand of Christianity formulated by Paul of Tarsus, that of universal salvation through faith in Christ's sacrifice on the cross, was challenged at every turn by other Christian factions, or "other Christianities" in the words of Bart Ehrman. Paramount among these were Gnostic Christians who had different ideas about Jesus' teachings, and what they meant for the people of the Roman Empire.

From the fourth century onward, the very nature of Jesus' divinity, as the Son of God, became the subject of a fierce debate that literally ripped the nascent Church apart, producing factions such as Arianism, Monophysitism and Nestorianism. As we will see, the divisions were brought into sharp relief with the rising conflict between the Western and the Eastern Church, and ultimately created the Great Schism of 1054. Five centuries later, Western Europe was torn in half when Martin Luther denounced the papacy for its exploitation of the faithful and launched the Reformation.[3]

In America, differences between various Christian factions were seeded almost from the beginning. The New England

Colonies had sprung from a variety of English religious groups, including Quaker and Puritan sects, with the specific purpose of creating an egalitarian society based on strict religious values. The South, on the other hand, retained much of the class distinctions that had ruled society in Great Britain. Its landed gentry, about 5 percent of the population, owned vast plantations and controlled much of the political, social, and religious scene, including the power to appoint local Anglican ministers. By contrast, the Middle Colonies (including present-day New York, New Jersey, Pennsylvania, and Delaware) were more moderate in scope, arguably because of their mix of French, German, Irish, and English immigrants. These colonies nurtured a large and vibrant middle class of hard-working and fiercely independent tradesmen including toolmakers, tanners, butchers, brickmakers, carpenters, clockmakers, and fishermen, many of whom were either Catholic or Lutheran.

The nation's founding fathers, however, adhered to neither creed. Many of them were avowed Deists who believed that while God created the universe, He did not intervene in human affairs. It was therefore up to humankind, guided by rational thought, to create order in the chaos. In drafting the Constitution of the United States, for example, Jefferson and his fellow authors did not look to the Bible but to the tracts of the liberal Enlightenment, including Montesquieu's *De l'Esprit des Loix* ("The Spirit of Laws," 1748).[4] Thus was born the first nation on earth to be governed by the idea that every citizen had certain inalienable rights, including the right to life, liberty, property, and worship, provided it did not trespass on the rights of others.

The religious differences between the colonies mattered little while they fought a bitter war to achieve their independence from Great Britain. But the wholesale destruction of churches during the American Revolution, combined with a "brain drain" of Methodist and Anglican clergy who fled back to the English mother country, created a religious vacuum. This prompted the rise of a new and indigenous form of American Christianity: of believers who met in tents or camps using a largely improvised combination of prayer, preaching, and hymns. Freed from the doctrinal debate that characterized European Christianity, the simple joy of communal singing and prayer gave these congregations a unique sense of personal empowerment. Like the frontiersmen of decades past, these worshippers felt as if they stood on the cusp of a new discovery, a spiritual experience on distinctly American terms. Thus was born a unique American faith tradition: that of *Evangelicalism*, based on the vision that America's destiny lay in becoming a Christian nation of impeccable moral and spiritual standards. The revivalist mood produced a number of other offshoots, most notably the Church of Jesus Christ of Latter-Day Saints in the Midwest and the Baptist confession in the South.

In the nineteenth century, however, the issue of slavery drove a new wedge through American Christianity. Presbyterians, Baptists, and Methodists all split when their southern members refused to denounce slavery as their northern counterparts did. The wounds of those years were not healed until the late twentieth century; some believe they were never healed at all.

At the dawn of the 1900s, America's religious map changed once more when waves of immigrants tripled the number of Catholics in the country. This prompted the formation of groups like the Ku Klux Klan, which actively promoted discrimination against Catholics, Jews, and African Americans. In response, the political ruling class organized itself around mainline Protestant churches that preached temperance in doctrine and moderation on social issues. As Ross Douthat recently wrote, between 1877 and 1961 there were thirteen mainline-affiliated presidents, ending with Dwight Eisenhower.[5]

From the 1970s onward, the role of moderate, centrist Protestantism in American society began to change. This was fueled in part by a new movement to align conservative Baptists, Catholics, and Evangelicals with a political agenda to ban abortion, to deny state recognition of same-sex relationships, and to advance Creationist education and prayer in public schools. At the same time, some on the extreme left were drawn to the so-called liberation theology then emerging in Latin America. Faced with the oppression by dictators in the region, many liberation theologists believed that the Gospel could be harmonized with Marxist-inspired resistance.

Within the Catholic Church, the focus on sexual mores drove an even deeper divide, notwithstanding efforts by Pope Francis to redirect the Church to the urgent social issues of our day. The rift between progressive and conservative Christians was further deepened during and after the Trump Administration. In the 2020 election, religious orientation proved to be a greater indicator of voting preferences than at any time in the post-war era. For example, 81 percent of white voters who describe themselves as evangelical or born-again Christians voted for Trump, according to an Associated Press survey, compared to 18 percent who voted for Biden. Edison Research estimate that the split was 76 percent for Trump and 24 percent for Biden.[6] By comparison, the vote in 2016 among white evangelicals was 80 percent for Trump and 16 percent for Hillary Clinton.

Even Catholic voters showed in 2020 an almost even split between the Catholic candidate and the non-observant one: 49

percent voted for Biden and 50 percent voted for Trump. This suggests that white voters with a strong Christian faith continued to support Trump despite his personal moral flaws and policies that favored the wealthy top one percent. The critical factor here was undoubtedly Trump's effort to appoint conservative judges to the Supreme Court who, in 2022, would overturn Roe vs. Wade.

It is therefore not surprising that today, American Christianity is on the verge of a veritable schism along the fault lines of the nation's culture wars.

How can we make sense of this? How can each side, whether liberal or conservative, claim to follow in the footsteps of Jesus? And how can Christians come together to heal this great divide, and together rebuild our nation as Jesus showed us?

The answer, as argued in this book, is simple: by returning to the very ideas that Jesus articulated throughout his ministry. I decided to write this book because we no longer talk much about those ideas. For many Christians, particularly conservatives and Evangelicals, the principal function of Jesus' ministry was his death on the cross and subsequent resurrection, so as to redeem all of humankind. That, of course, is the essential focus of the *Pauline kerygma*, the belief system developed by Paul in his efforts to convert the vast masses of Gentiles in Asia Minor (modern Turkey) and beyond. Paul never met Jesus, was never witness to his powerful oratory, nor did he actively engage with the Apostles who had been with Jesus throughout his ministry. As a result, what actually happened during the relatively brief period of Jesus' ministry—a timespan of some eighteen months, to judge by the Synoptic Gospels—often receives short shrift. But by ignoring the things that Jesus talked about, we ignore the very essence of his movement, and what prompted him to become an activist rabbi or "teacher" to begin with.

In fact, as this book will try to show, Jesus' ministry unfolded in a crisis very similar to the one we are battling today. The daily news feed of thousands of people who are out of work, battling chronic illness, facing eviction, or struggling to feed their families, is a world Jesus would have recognized. That is because Jesus' teachings were framed by the truly catastrophic conditions of early first-century Galilee. Though few people realize it today, the Galilee of Jesus' time was a land devastated by a punishing tax regimen levied by the Herodian dynasty, which prompted two peasant revolts when Jesus was a young boy. As we will see, the ultimate purpose of this tax yoke was to evict the Galilean peasants from their landholdings, so that these could be combined into vast estates or *agroi* as Mark, Matthew and Luke call them, tended by hired stewards or *oikonomoi*.

Only in this manner could King Herod produce the large quantities of export products, including cereals and olive oil, that were prized throughout the Roman Empire. In turn, the proceeds of this export surplus allowed him to satisfy his zest for large building projects, including Roman-style cities such as Sebaste and Caesarea Maritima, and fortresses like Masada and the Herodion.

In response, Jesus formulated a unique vision that he called the "Kingdom of God" (or in the case of Matthew, the "Kingdom of Heaven," which piously avoids the name of the Divine). At its core, this vision was a blueprint for a social and spiritual renewal of the Jewish nation, as described in Jesus' famous Sermon of the Mount. For Jesus, the Kingdom was not a political construct but a new way in which society would operate, based on the three quintessential pillars of the Torah:

social justice; compassion toward one another; and an abiding love of God. Unlike John the Baptist, who argued that Israel could only be redeemed through regime change, Jesus believed that a grassroots movement of people power would make this Kingdom a reality.

If that is the case, then how can we return to the essential precepts of Jesus' Kingdom vision? How can we set our doctrinal differences aside and together, as Christians, embrace the core teachings that Jesus left us?

Here, too, the answer is straightforward, for Jesus left us a prayer that articulates the key precepts of the Kingdom in terms that his followers among the Galilean fishermen and peasantry could understand. That prayer is known as the Lord's Prayer, or more informally, the *Our Father*. Its verses have formed the wellspring of Christian faith from the very beginning. As word of Jesus' ministry spread throughout the Mediterranean world, followers continued to recite it, which is how it found its way into the Gospels. Even as the early Church grew across the Roman Empire and into foreign lands never touched by Roman culture, the prayer often served as a vanguard. Especially in places where no one spoke Greek or Latin, the *Our Father* was usually the first Christian text to be translated, long before the Gospels became available in the local tongue. For example, the first English version of the prayer was composed as early as 650 CE. The power of this prayer continues to this day. Although Christianity's 2.4 billion followers are splintered over countless traditions and sharply different views on doctrine, the one thing that all confessions share is the *Our Father*.

That is why, in addressing the urgent needs of our wounded nation, this book will take its cue from the tenets of the *Our Father*—the only doctrine that Christians agree on. In doing so, the book will first try to reconstruct Jesus' ministry, based on historical sources as well as the Gospels. We will then explore what Jesus meant with each prayer's verse, and how it illustrates a key element of his Kingdom of God philosophy. Finally, the book will try to reconstruct, hour by hour, the events that have defined Christianity: Jesus' Passion. And throughout, we will apply Jesus' ideas to our modern world, and show how these can guide us to build a more equal, compassionate, and loving society.

As Christians we can argue about many things. Across the centuries, we have allowed our doctrines and dogmas—whether on the left or the right—to diverge so much that we have lost sight of what Jesus' ministry was about, and what he taught us to do. That is partly due to the fact that his ministry was so short. So short, in fact, that written testimony of his teachings would not emerge until at least a generation later. What's more, those testimonies—the Gospels and other sources—all originated in different parts of the Roman Empire, written by scribes who historically were not eyewitnesses to the events themselves. That explains why the Gospels often provide different accounts about what took place during those pivotal months of Jesus' ministry, or what it is that Jesus tried to accomplish. Nevertheless, all Gospels agree on the purpose of Jesus' principal message: to build the Kingdom of God. Nowhere is that purpose more clearly stated than in the beautiful verses of the *Our Father*.

That is why this book will reach out to all Christians, regardless of their affiliation, by exploring the story behind each of the prayer's verses—and by showing how these can help us to restore our own world. But before we do that, let us first return to Galilee in the opening decades of the first century, and revisit the conditions that set the stage for Jesus' ministry.

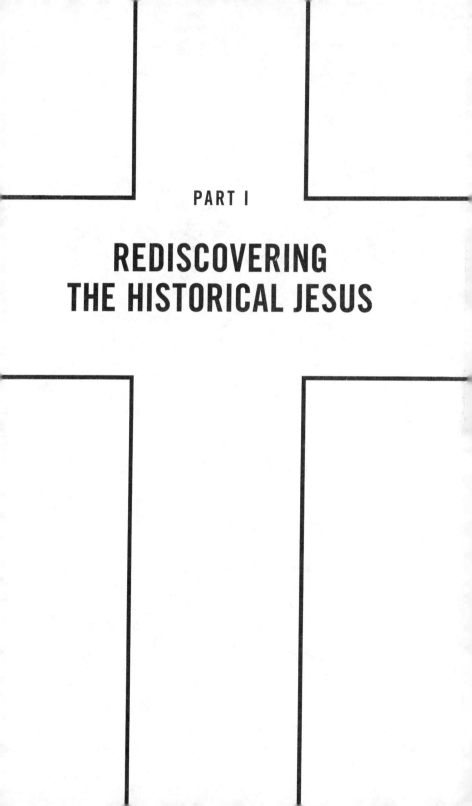

PART I

REDISCOVERING
THE HISTORICAL JESUS

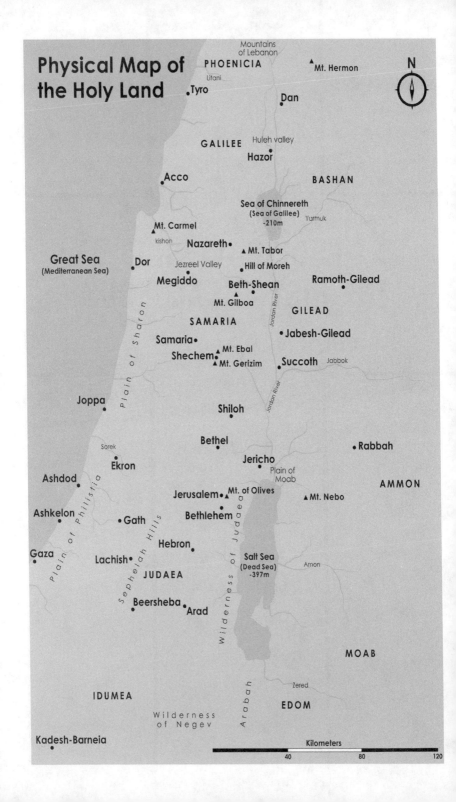

Physical Map of the Holy Land

N

PHOENICIA

Mountains of Lebanon

▲ Mt. Hermon

Litani

• Tyro

• Dan

GALILEE

Huleh valley

Hazor

• Acco

BASHAN

Sea of Chinnereth
(Sea of Galilee)
-210m

Yarmuk

▲ Mt. Carmel

kishon

Nazareth •

▲ Mt. Tabor

Great Sea
(Mediterranean Sea)

• Dor

Jezreel Valley

• Hill of Moreh

Megiddo

Beth-Shean

Ramoth-Gilead •

▲ Mt. Gilboa

SAMARIA

GILEAD

Samaria •

• Jabesh-Gilead

Shechem ▲ Mt. Ebal
▲ Mt. Gerizim

Succoth •

Jabbok

Plain of Sharon

Jordan River

Jordan River

• Joppa

Shiloh •

Bethel •

• Rabbah

Sorek

Jericho •

Ekron •

Plain of Moa

Ashdod •

AMMON

Jerusalem • ▲ Mt. of Olives

▲ Mt. Nebo

Ashkelon •

Bethlehem •

Plain of Philistia

• **Gath**

Sephelah Hills

Hebron •

Wilderness of Judaea

Salt Sea
(Dead Sea)
-397m

Gaza •

Lachish •

Amon

JUDAEA

Beersheba •
• **Arad**

MOAB

IDUMEA

Arabah

Zered

EDOM

Wilderness
of Negev

Kadesh-Barneia

Kilometers

40   80   120

| 1 |

A LAND IN CRISIS

What was it like to live in Galilee during the time of Jesus? To answer that question, the first thing we should remember is that Galileans were socially and culturally different from the heartland of the Jewish nation, called Judea. For much of the preceding ten centuries, Galilee had been a distinct political entity, which meant that Galileans spoke a different dialect, shared a different ancestry, and often hailed from a village culture that was distinct from those living in Samaria or Judea. That difference also extended to the geography of these regions. Whereas Judea consists of highlands and dry desert, Galilee was divided in two regions, Upper (or northern) Galilee and Lower (or southern) Galilee, following the natural contours of the land.

A land of tall peaks and deep valleys, Upper Galilee is a rugged country with limestone plateaus rising as high as 3,000 feet. Even today, its mountains serve as the region's principal source of water, enjoying a rainfall of as much as forty inches per year— far more than in any other part of Israel. Below the natural boundary of the HaKerem Valley is Lower Galilee, the place where Jesus lived as a young boy. It was a beautiful land, a veritable Garden of Eden filled with a range of flowers and plants, with manifold birds wheeling in the sky. "Its soil is so universally rich and fruitful, and so full of the plantations of trees of all sorts," the first-century historian Josephus wrote, "that it invites even the most indolent to engage in agriculture, because of its fruitfulness." The ridges surrounding the Geba'ot Allonim, for example, were covered with lush shrubs that thrived on the alluvial soil of chalk and limestone, while the hillsides teemed with dense brush and olive trees. In the east, however, the picture was different. Here were highlands made of basalt, and hills could stretch for miles without any prominent vegetation other than low-level brush and grass.

But the true secret of Galilee's fertility was its supply of water. In the region around the escarpment now known as the Nazareth Ridge, natural springs such as the Nahal Sippori provided a stable source of water all year round. These springs were fed by large subterranean aquifers of cool water, which made the region uniquely suited for the cultivation of fruits and vegetables. The bountiful presence of water and the outstanding quality of the soil guaranteed that the area around the Nazareth Ridge would attract the greatest density of settlement from the Early Iron Age and well into the Roman era. In fact, it is from Galilee that we have one of the earliest written testimonies of human habitation in Israel—or Canaan, as it was called—before the days of Joshua's conquest.

At the same time, though, Galilee found itself politically isolated on almost all sides. To the northwest was the Phoenician region of Sidon and Tyre, which served as the main conduit of Greek cultural influence extending well into the days of Jesus. To

| *A View of the Sea of Galilee near Tabgha, Israel.*

the northeast was the land of Aram-Damascus, and to the east lay the territory of Ammon and Moab (today's Jordan). Galilee was therefore an enclave of sorts, insular and landlocked, though with access to the Sea of Galilee. In sum, it formed an almost perfect circle of highly fertile land surrounded by foreigners—which is probably the root of the word Galilee (*ha-galil*), based on the Hebrew *galil ha-goyim,* meaning "circle of the peoples."

During the days of Israel's independence, the Northern Kingdom (as distinct from its southern neighbor, the Kingdom of Judah) focused on exploiting Galilee's rich agricultural soil, producing olive oil, wine, figs, dates, and grains. The result was a growing agricultural surplus that boosted trade with surrounding regions.[1] But after the Assyrian invasions, Galilee was broken up into separate provinces and heavily colonized by Assyrian—and later, Babylonian—settlers. Recent archaeological surveys have shown that by the eighth century BCE, much of Lower Galilee had suffered a considerable interruption in existing population patterns as a result of eager Assyrian settlers.[2] As Isaiah wrote, "[The Lord] brought into contempt the land of Zebulun and the land of Naphtali" (Isaiah 9:1). Even during the Persian period, when King Cyrus the Great granted Judah—now named *Yehud*—a large measure of autonomy to be ruled by its priestly elite, the province of Galilee remained a satrapy under full control of its Persian overlords. Worse, when Galilee became part of the Seleucid Empire in the wake of the conquests by Alexander the Great, Jewish farmers had, in fact, become a *minority*. According to the book of 1 Maccabees, a number of the local Gentiles set out to erase the Jewish presence in Galilee altogether.[3]

In the process, what had once been a predominantly Israelite region became a patchwork of cultures. That made Galileans suspect in the eyes of the "pure" Jews of Judah, a prejudice that extended well into the time of Jesus. This explains why the Gospel of Matthew still refers to the region as the "Galilee of the Gentiles" and why, in the Gospel of John, one of the Apostles' friends would scoff, *Nazareth?* "Can any good come out of Nazareth?" (Matthew 4:15; John 1:46). Galilee, in sum, was not the type of place where pious Judeans expected to find a *hasid* or "holy man" like Jesus. Scores of coins and pottery fragments of Greek origin, brought to light in recent excavations, show that even in the time of Jesus, Galilee was a patchwork of both Jewish and Gentile enclaves. Townships could have a mixed population of both Jews and Gentiles, whereas cities like Scythopolis (the biblical Beth Shean) and Tiberias were overwhelmingly Gentile. Only rural villages remained Jewish in name and observance. Josephus tells us that there were no fewer than 204 such hamlets, most clinging tenaciously to their ancestral Jewish faith and customs, even as the world around them became first a Greek and then a Roman preserve.

During the Hasmonean Restoration (142–63 BCE), when the historical land of Israel once again achieved its independence, Galilean farmers were largely left in peace to cultivate their lands. But that changed when the last Hasmonean ruler, Queen Alexandra, died in 67 BCE and a civil war erupted between her sons Hyrcanus II and Aristobulus II, each vying for the throne. The turmoil of that period soon came to the attention of the Roman general Pompey. He and his armies had arrived in the Middle East for the purpose of ending the Third Mithridatic War (73–63 BCE). Rome was now the undisputed master of the Eastern Mediterranean and used every means at its disposal to enforce the *Pax Romana,* the Roman Peace, so that trade could flourish and grain ships could make their way to Rome. Little surprise, then, that Pompey was deeply disturbed by the brewing trouble in the Hasmonean Kingdom. He decided to put an end to it by conquering the region and making it a vassal state of Rome. Thus, the ancient land of Israel became a Roman possession, with Hyrcanus II as its puppet king.

In due course, the largely inept Hyrcanus appointed a talented manager to administer this vassal kingdom, and his name was Antipater. That Antipater hailed from Idumea (roughly the territory of today's Negev Desert) and remained an Arab pagan at heart did not bother Hyrcanus in the least. Ruling the kingdom in all but name, Antipater decided to appoint his sons as governors (or *strategoi*) of the kingdom. It so happened that the young man placed in charge of Galilee was a son named Herod. Like his father, Herod had no particular love for the Jewish people or its customs, but he did nurture a fierce ambition to make his mark on the region by ingratiating himself with the ruling Romans.

Herod soon saw his opportunity when civil war broke out in Rome after the assassination of Julius Caesar. One of the assassins, Cassius, desperately needed to raise an army to defend himself and appealed to Herod's father, Antipater, for a huge sum of money—seven hundred talents—or some six million dollars in today's currency. Antipater turned to his sons to raise these funds. Herod eagerly accepted the assignment and squeezed the Galilean peasants with ruinous taxes until they produced the needed cash: 350 talents, or some three million dollars. Farmers unable to pay the tribute were sold into slavery. Not surprisingly, Herod's regime prompted a resistance movement led by a man named Hezekiah, who may have been a member of the old Hasmonean nobility. From a historical perspective, this was rather unprecedented; Galilee had always been a relatively peaceful region, compared to its restless southern neighbor Judea. According to Josephus, the revolt was bloodily suppressed and scores of people were killed in the process.

In the eyes of Rome, the fact that Herod had Galilean blood on his hands did not disqualify him in the least as a candidate to rule all of Roman Palestine. On the contrary, when in 40 BCE the Parthians invaded the region and Rome feared a disruption to its bread supply, the Roman Senate was more than happy to elevate Herod and crown him king. They even provided him with legions to oust the Parthians and pacify the kingdom. Roman senators liked having a vassal king who could be relied upon to keep his restive people under control, and to pay his annual tribute on time. Thus, the reign of Herod the Great (37–4 BCE) began.

But Herod soon discovered what his father Antipater must have known all along: the heartland of Judea was an extremely poor country. Unlike Spain, it had no silver or tin mines; unlike northern Africa, it lacked any gold deposits; unlike Gaul, the Balkans, or Lebanon, it lacked dense forests that could feed the Empire's appetite for construction and shipbuilding. As Josephus put it, "we neither inhabit a maritime country, nor do we delight in merchandise . . . (but) having a fruitful country for our habitation, we take pains in cultivating that only."[4] In other words, the only resource the region did have were its fertile valleys in the north that had always been the breadbasket of the Middle East with its production of wheat, barley, olives, figs, and dates.

But Herod wasn't interested in ruling a poor country. Like other kingdoms along the Eastern Mediterranean, he wanted to build *poleis* or cities in the Greco-Roman style to please his master, Emperor Augustus. Augustus believed that the only way the growing Roman Empire could prosper and endure was if its territory was ruled by Roman law, if all commerce was done with Roman currency, and if all of its principal cities were beautified in the Greco-Roman style, with forums, temples, bathhouses, and marketplaces.

The problem was, to build such cities from scratch was a very expensive proposition. Where would Herod find the money to do so? The answer, as in the case of Cassius' army, was obvious: by taxing the only resource of value in the kingdom, the agriculture of Galilee, to the limit. Except, this time Herod went a step further. He was no longer content to squeeze the Galilean peasants dry with his taxes; he wanted their *land*. The reason is that there was something peculiar about Galilean cultivation that he had noticed when he served as the region's governor: its

Scythopolis, the biblical Beth Shean, was the only polis *or Greek-style city of the Decapolis to be located west of the Jordan River.*

agriculture was fragmented and inefficient. Land parcels were typically passed from generation to generation, and then often divided among the sons, or used as a dowry for daughters. That meant that Galilean plots were small, and barely sufficient for subsistence farming—the practice of growing a variety of small crops just to feed a family, including cereals, legumes, olives, and perhaps some grapes. Any surplus that might be left over was considered a bonus and was usually sold at the local market, or bartered for other goods.

Archaeological evidence bears this out. Records such as the Zenon Papyri, compiled around 220 BCE, indicate that the average private land holding was four to eight acres. That fits with Roman records: Julius Caesar gave his veterans a plot of ten *jugura,* the equivalent of six acres, which was considered the very minimum with which a retired soldier could sustain a family with three children.[5] A United Nations survey of Southeast Asia recently concluded that some 60 percent of rural families possess no more than five acres of land, which, even using modern seeds and fertilizers, produces subsistence yields barely sufficient to feed an average family with four or five children.[6]

In other words, the peasantry of Galilee lived on a knife's edge of survival. As subsistence farmers, they had no room for error, particularly because the Torah, the Jewish law, expected a farmer to pay a tithe. The basis for this tithing was the belief that the land belonged to Yahweh, and that the Israelites were merely tenant farmers, tilling the land at the Lord's pleasure. Therefore, it was only proper that a share of the harvest should be returned to its rightful owner. As a result, ten percent of the harvest had to be donated to the priests and priestly assistants known as the Levites. In addition, farmers had to pay a Temple tax of half a shekel, which was the equivalent of a worker's wages for two days.

Knowing this, Herod came up with a devious plan. He believed that if all these hundreds of tiny peasant plots were consolidated into large estates, run by professional stewards, he could achieve a vast increase in the yields of the most desirable crops, to be sold on the markets of the Roman global economy. After all, that is why he had wanted to build a large port, Caesarea Maritima, to begin with; there was no point in having a large modern harbor if you had no export to sell.

The mechanism to accomplish this mass eviction of the Galilean peasantry was Herod's tried and true method: weaponized taxation. Richard Horsley, who made a detailed study of the Herodian tax regime in the decades before and after the birth of Jesus, has argued that farmers went from a single layer of taxation during the Hasmonean period—payable to the ruling monarchy—to a double layer of taxes during the Herodian Era, both to pay the tribute to Rome and to fund Herod's lavish lifestyle and building mania.[7] And this, we should remember, came on top of the tithes and offerings to the Temple and the priesthood.

In addition, life in Galilee was further burdened by a salt tax, custom duties for the shipment of produce from one region to the next, tax on property, fishing polls, and tax on other sources of "manufacturing," notably the production of salted fish. For Herod, Galilee was a colony, pure and simple, and like any other colony its primary purpose was to be exploited for the greater good of Rome and that of its vassal king. Scholars such as E. P. Sanders have estimated that as much as 33 percent of a farmer's harvest was now earmarked for the combined demands of taxes and tithing. Horsley believes it was even higher, closer to 40 percent. When you factor in the frequency of poor harvests due to drought, pests, or banditry, this tax burden became entirely unsustainable.[8]

But that was the whole point of Herod's plan. He knew that in order to meet this impossible tax yoke, farmers needed to borrow, and borrow heavily. It so happened that the only people with the capital to provide loans were also the people responsible for collecting the taxes to begin with: the *telonai*, as the Gospels call them, or "tax collectors." In the Gospel of Luke, we learn of debtors who owed their creditors the staggering amount of "fifty measures of oil" or "fourscore measures of wheat," suggesting interest rates of anywhere between 25 and 50 percent (Luke 7:41; 16:1–13). And when, inevitably, the loan became due and the farmer was unable to pay it, the tax collectors moved in and confiscated his land.

This explains why these tax collectors, these "publicans," are so despised in the Gospels, and why the people are so surprised when Jesus decides to break bread with them, as we will see later on. Acting on orders from the Herodian regime, they were responsible for thousands of Galilean farmers and their families becoming homeless, dispossessed, and without the means to support themselves.

The opportunity to buy land cheap from bankrupt farmers soon attracted a new class of *nouveaux riches,* officials or cronies of Herod's court, who wasted no time in building and enlarging their estates. The essential difference between them and the old landed Hasmonean aristocracy was that these *arrivistes* actively supported Herod and Roman rule. Consequently, these landowners, many of them Judeans, were not burdened by any sentimental feelings toward the Galilean peasantry. They gladly took control of the confiscated plots, small though they may have been, and offered the unfortunate farmers work as tenants, cultivating the land they had once owned for the wages of a day laborer.

Part of my decades-long research into the historical Jesus was motivated by this simple question: why are the pages of the Gospels filled with thousands of homeless, hungry and diseased people, even though they're living in one of the most fertile lands in the Middle East? Why does this vast Galilean proletariat form the principal audience for Jesus' sermons, in contrast to the soldiers, officials, Sadducees, Pharisees, and other members of the elite who flocked to hear John the Baptist speak? And why has no one ever addressed this question in depth, particularly because so much of Jesus' words and deeds are focused on alleviating the suffering of the Galilean people?

Well, this is the answer. The fact of the matter is that Jesus' ministry unfolded in a time of unprecedented social and economic disruption, producing a vast gap between the rich elite and the vast majority of the poor and dispossessed. I believe that, in many ways, it was these terrible conditions that not only informed but also prompted and even shaped Jesus' ministry. That in itself makes Jesus' teachings so eminently relevant for us in the second decade of the twenty-first century, when we ourselves witness the fall-out from our growing inequality and the yawning gap between a tiny elite and a vast majority of American citizens struggling to get by.

In the face of the growing opposition to his regime and the rising hatred of his Jewish subjects, Herod first tried to mollify the people by building a vast expansion of the Temple in Jerusalem, which scholars refer to as the "Second Temple" after the first sanctuary was destroyed by the Babylonian King Nebuchadnezzar in 586 BCE. Since the Temple area was perched on a hill known as Temple Mount, Herod's architects first created an artificial plateau supported by massive walls. The Western Wall in Jerusalem, which today is the holiest place of Judaism, is in fact one of these mammoth Herodian supporting

A model of the Second Temple sanctuary based on plans conceived by Herod the Great. The Temple was probably completed in 62 CE and destroyed only eight years later.

walls. This huge esplanade was accessible through two staircases on the west, each supported by arches. A small portion of one of these arches, known as Robinson's Arch, is still visible today, as are the monumental stairs that led to the Double Gate on the east. Construction on the Temple expansion was begun in 22 BCE and was still ongoing when Jesus visited the Temple during Passover of 30 CE.

Before long, however, Herod began to suspect opposition and conspiracies against his rule at every turn. In response, he created a police state not unlike the autocratic regimes of our own times. Prominent officials and citizens were ordered to swear an oath of allegiance to the king. Everyone arousing even the slightest suspicion was closely watched by Herod's secret police. Citizens were encouraged to inform on one another; "even in the cities and on the open roads, there were men who spied on those who met together," says Josephus. Dissidents were caught and "disappeared"—they were dispatched to concentration centers in Herod's fortresses (as John the Baptist was) and executed without trial.[9]

Herod's vast construction program and the growing trade with surrounding states may have created a boom economy, but it was a short-lived prosperity that mostly benefited the upper crust of Jewish society: the merchants, the priestly elite of the Sadducees, and Herodian officials eager to collaborate with the Roman occupiers. Beneath the Herodian veneer of Hellenistic gentility, the country seethed with unrest—which, as we will see, would erupt shortly after the birth of Jesus. We can get an idea of the extent of Herod's rapacious regime when we consider the fabulous fortune Herod had managed to amass near the end of his life. As Josephus reports, Herod bequeathed the staggering sum of ten million *drachmae* to his mentor and protector, Emperor Augustus (one drachma, a Greek coin, was worth approximately $0.65 in biblical times). In addition, he gave gold, silver, and precious garments to Augustus' wife, Livia, as well as another five million drachmae to "certain others," no doubt Roman officials, prelates, and military leaders to whom Herod owed some favors. Even then, he still had sufficient capital to grant his sister Salome five hundred thousand drachmae, while also giving the rest of his surviving kin "sums of money . . . that left them all in a wealthy condition."[10] This, we should remember, was the fortune that remained *after* Herod had expended a good deal of his treasure on massive projects, including the construction of Caesarea, the acropolis of Sebaste on the ancient site of Samaria, and the expansion of the Second Temple.

In 4 BCE, King Herod finally died after a long and painful illness. Based on the reports from Josephus, modern physicians have tried to determine exactly what ailed the king, but the data is scant. A chronic kidney ailment has been suggested, based on symptoms described by Josephus, also because Herod's grandson Agrippa I died of a similar affliction in 44 CE. But Herod's family made sure that the old king was buried with the most dazzling splendor anyone in Judea had ever seen. The funeral cortege was led by the king's magnificent hearse, covered from top to bottom in billowing brocades of gold that glistened in the sun. Inside lay the king's body wrapped in folds of imperial purple. His cold fingers, studded with precious gems and stones, still clasped the scepter of his office, while his head proudly bore the crown that had once been bestowed by Augustus himself. Right behind the carriage came Herod's immediate family– that is to say, those who were fortunate enough to have survived his murderous reign. First came his son Archelaus, believed by many to be his heir, accompanied by his siblings: his younger brother Antipas, his half-brother Philip, and his half-sister Salome, all dressed in somber clothes of mourning. They were followed by Herod's mounted Royal Guards, wearing polished breastplates and plumed helmets that flashed in the sun. Lastly, the long train was closed by the more than five hundred officials, servants, and domestics who had served the king during his lifetime.

For hours on end, the procession marched on, steadily winding through the hills of the Judean Desert to their final destination: the fortress of Herodion. Here, in years past, the king had built an elaborate palace complex. As the sarcophagus was opened and his body was slowly lowered in its rose-colored tomb, many felt as if the sun was setting on one of the most magnificent epochs in Judea's long history. But no one realized that the old king had one last surprise in store.

Meanwhile, up north, in a small hamlet in Galilee, a young toddler had just begun to walk.

The author with the sarcophagus, excavated at the Herodium in 2010, which is believed to have held the remains of Herod the Great.

THE LOST YEARS OF
JESUS' YOUTH

Our primary sources about the early years of Jesus are the Nativity narratives in the Gospels of Matthew and Luke. A principal focus of these narratives is the need to situate Jesus' birth in Bethlehem, a village outside of Jerusalem in Judea, rather than in Nazareth. Matthew, in fact, is quite up-front about this prerequisite, because that is how Jesus could qualify as the Messiah, the Jewish Redeemer, as foretold in a prophesy by the Prophet Micah. Matthew even paraphrases Micah's prophecy in full:

And you, Bethlehem, in the land of Judah,
are by no means least among the rulers of Judah;
for from you shall come a ruler
who is to shepherd my people in Israel.
(Matthew 2:6, paraphrasing Micah 5:2 and 2 Samuel 5:2)

This is why both Matthew and Luke look for a way to move the birth of Jesus from Nazareth to Bethlehem, even though both Gospels, independent of each other, arrive at different scenarios to make that happen.

Luke, who is more concerned about the historical context of his story than any of the other evangelists, uses the Roman census ordered by the governor of Syria, Quirinius, to get the couple to Judea. He writes:

> In those days a decree went out from Emperor Augustus that all the world should be registered. This was the first registration and was taken while Quirinius was governor of Syria. All went to their own towns to be registered. Joseph also went from the town of Nazareth in Galilee to Judea, to the city of David called Bethlehem, because he was descended from the house and family of David. (Luke 2:1–4)

At first glance, this statement seems plausible. After 6 CE, Judea became a crown province of Rome, rather than an autonomous region. Its ruler, a Roman prefect appointed by the emperor, had a direct reporting line to Quirinius, the governor of Greater Syria, based in the Syrian capital of Antioch. And there was indeed a census organized by Quirinius at that time. The problem is that this census did not take place until ten years after the birth of Jesus.

The second issue is that the purpose of a Roman census was not to count the population but to establish the value of the tax base in that region. That became an urgent question after Judea became a Roman possession, which meant that collecting the annual tribute was now a Roman responsibility, using the *telonai*, the middlemen who served as tax collectors. The purpose of the census, therefore, was to establish the net worth of the property of those who happened to live in Judea at that time. To do that, the Romans wanted the people to stay *in their homes,* where the tax man could find them, rather than in the place of their ancestors.

For these two reasons, then, the census would not have applied to Jesus' parents, whom the Gospels identify as *Yosef* or Joseph, and *Maryam* or Mary. One, because their place of residence was Nazareth in Galilee, rather than in Judea; and two, because unlike Judea, Galilee was still an autonomous province and therefore exempt from the Roman census. And finally, in that year of 6 CE, Jesus was already at least ten years old.

Matthew, however, resolves the problem of getting Mary and Joseph into Bethlehem in a more straightforward manner. Whereas Luke's Nativity story is told from Mary's point of

The Ahenobarbus relief depicts a Roman census around the second century BCE.

view—including the Annunciation by the Angel Gabriel—
Matthew's story is narrated from Joseph's perspective. He writes:

> The three wise men set out; and there, ahead of them, went
> the star that they had seen at its rising, until it stopped over
> the place where the child was. When they saw that the star
> had stopped, they were overwhelmed with joy. On entering
> the house, they saw the child with Mary his mother; and
> they knelt down and paid him homage. (Matthew 2:9–11)

In Matthew's version, therefore, there is no stable, no child in
the manger, and no shepherds in the fields. Instead, Matthew
quite deliberately uses the Greek word *oikia* for "the house"
where the three wise men found Mary and the baby Jesus. *Oikia*
means a place of residence, a home. In other words, Matthew
says that Mary and Joseph were actually *living* in Bethlehem
when Mary gave birth to her child. It is only after Herod's
massacre of the newborn children in Bethlehem (an event not
reported by Josephus) that the family flees to Egypt, and then
decides to move to Nazareth in Galilee, rather than returning
to their homestead in Bethlehem. The reason, says Matthew,
is that Joseph heard that King Herod was dead and that Judea
was now ruled by his son Archelaus. Then, at the end of both
infancy narratives, both Matthew and Luke continue the story
in the village of Nazareth.

The scholar Bruce Chilton has argued another possibility.[1]
Seven miles northwest of Nazareth, in the heart of Galilee, was
a small village that was also called Bethlehem, or "Bethlehem-
in-Galilee." It is listed among nineteen names in Joshua's
description of the boundaries of the tribe of Zebulun (Joshua
19:15). The presence of a village named Bethlehem in such close

proximity to Nazareth could suggest that this is the place where Mary went to give birth, away from the wagging tongues of her home town, precisely because her pregnancy was under a cloud of uncertain paternity; she had conceived the child by the Holy Spirit before Joseph and she were wed. The putative birth of Jesus in a *Galilean* village called Bethlehem may have inspired the evangelists to link it to Micah's prophesy.

For seven days after the birth of her male child, Mary was considered ritually impure (Leviticus 12:2). This enabled her body to recover from the strains of childbirth. If her baby had been a daughter, the period of impurity would have been 14 days (Leviticus 2:5). Then, on the eighth day after birth, the baby Jesus was considered strong enough to undergo *berit,* or ritual circumcision (Genesis 17:10–12). "After eight days had passed," Luke says, "it was time to circumcise the child" (Luke 2:21).

| *A reconstruction of a Jewish home in the village of Qatzrin, Upper Galilee*

This ritual usually took place with all the family and all the elders present. According to ancient Jewish practice, Joseph marked this moment by naming the child. By doing so, Joseph accepted the child as his legitimate offspring.

The name he chose for his newborn son was Jesus or *Y'shua* in Aramaic, a very common name in first-century Palestine, perhaps comparable to the popularity of "John" or "Joe" in our modern day. In the works by Josephus, there appear at least twenty different men who are alternatively called "Jesus" or a variation thereof, "Joshua"—ten of whom are Jesus' contemporaries. *Y'shua*, a contraction of *Yehoshua*, is believed to mean "Yahweh is salvation."

Once the circumcision and naming ritual was completed, a feast was held to welcome the baby into the village community. The women set up tables laden with fruits, barley cakes, and wine. If the harvest had been good and plentiful, perhaps a lamb or a sheep would have been slaughtered to heighten the festivities.

And then, Mary and Joseph settled down to raise their child, which in first-century Galilee was beset by challenges, as we saw in the previous chapter. For the vast majority of men and women, life was a daily struggle for water, food, and shelter; for vouchsafing the harvest and caring for the herds, while worrying about the threat of drought, floods, wild animals, or hostile clans and thieves. There was little or no protection from the state, even though the state—in this case the Galilean administration of Herod's son, the *tetrarch* ("ruler of a fourth") Antipas—taxed its subjects mercilessly. Moreover, there was no social mobility to speak of. Most people lived within the constraints of their social condition, rarely straying from their place of birth, yet devoted to their families, their honor, and their faith.

Perhaps it is precisely because of the harsh setting of their lives that faith played such an important role. In our modern day, many of us tend to relegate faith to specific times or functions, such as saying grace before meals, going to worship in a synagogue or church, or celebrating a wedding. In biblical times, by contrast, faith and observance permeated almost everything people did. It was the precariousness of their existence that brought people closer to God. Only about half of all newborns, on average, lived to adulthood. One or two out of every five women died in childbirth. Disease was often a death sentence, for modern medicine did not exist. Even then, a war, a revolt, or a drought could wipe out entire families at a stroke. As a result, men and women in biblical times had a much more intuitive grasp of their spiritual lives; they had no cell phones to distract them from their inner selves. They *lived* their spirituality in the truest sense of the word—not only because the boundaries between family, work, and faith were far more blurred than today, but also because all was governed by the Torah, the corpus of Jewish Law.

And yet, the people of the Bible faced issues that are just as important today: how to keep their families safe; how to share resources equitably and fairly; how to live peacefully with other communities; how to resolve conflict; and how to live happy and honest lives. That is why the Bible, and particularly the Gospels, are as relevant as a moral compass today as they were in the time they were written.

The essential elements of home life in biblical lands changed little over the course of the millennium between the Davidic kingdom and the time of Jesus, and the same was true for the small family living in a hamlet called Nazareth. Daily life revolved primarily around the procurement of food and clean water, which most families obtained from their plots of land, their orchards, their livestock, and any nearby springs, cisterns, or wells. A spring is a spontaneous source of water near the surface, whereas a well is often dug deep into the soil to reach the water table beneath. Cisterns are large underground reservoirs lined with plaster to catch and hold rainwater. Of all these three water sources, the village well was the most ubiquitous. Because of its primary role in daily life, it was also the principal meeting spot where villagers congregated to socialize, gossip, or join in worship on the Sabbath.

Mark tells us that Joseph made a living as a carpenter. When the people of Nazareth were astounded by Jesus' preaching, they asked, "Is this not the carpenter, the son of Mary and brother of James?" (Mark 6:3). The problem with the traditional English translation of Mark's Greek text is that the Greek word *tektōn,* which the King James Bible translated as "carpenter," actually means something else: a skilled worker in either stone, wood, or metal. Other than olive wood, which is too gnarly, good workable wood was rare in Galilee, so wooden furniture—with the exception of farming tools or other simple stools—was beyond the reach of most peasants. What's more, when Jesus speaks in parables, he doesn't refer to woodworking at all, even though the sawing, drilling, and hammering of a workshop would have offered plenty of allegorical material. Instead, he always uses the vocabulary of agriculture.

Time and again, we hear Jesus talk about seeds and sowing, about the joys of a full orchard, or the frantic urgency of harvest time. Luke, for example, quotes the parable of a gardener who told the owner of a fig tree to "let it alone for one more year, until I dig around it and put manure on it. If it bears fruit next year, well and good; but if not, you should cut it down" (Luke 13:6–8). This sounds like a man who was very familiar with the rhythm of cultivation, observed during the seasonal cycles of orchards and fields.

There is a simple solution to this dilemma, which is that Joseph was both: a farmer who sustained his family with a small plot of land, and a skilled worker, an artisan, who complemented his income from the fields by crafting tools, carving stone or cutting tree branches as timber for roofs. If that assumption is correct, then Jesus' youth would have been governed by the same cycle of seasons that every other Galilean farmer was familiar with. Joseph would have started to prepare the soil for seeding in the month of Tishri (September–October) or Marchesvan (October–November). Jesus would have helped his father to clear the ground of rocks and other obstacles to get it ready for plowing. Joseph would then take a sack of seeds culled from the previous harvest and walk in straight lines across his land, throwing the seed with the full sweep of his arms. The young Jesus must have watched his father doing this, for years later it inspired his parable of the sower: "Some [seed] fell on the path, and the birds came and ate them up. Other seeds fell on rocky ground. . . . Other seeds fell on the good soil and brought forth grain, some a hundredfold, some sixty, some thirty" (Matthew 13:4–8).

This had been the rhythm of life for farmers since the earliest days of the Israelite monarchy, even during times of Assyrian, Persian, Greek, and now, Roman occupation. But in 4 BCE, something happened that would completely upstage Mary and Joseph's tranquil life in Galilee—and that of their newborn son.

We have to remember that the ancient world was a place without television, newspapers, social media, or the Internet.

The fertile valleys of Galilee in springtime, when the fields explode in a riot of colors.

There was only one way in which news could be transmitted, and that was by the spoken word. That is why travelers were often quizzed by local people when they passed through, because that was the only way they could find out what had happened beyond the horizon of their village. And so, word must have filtered down to Nazareth that the despised King Herod had died in 4 BCE. In the short term, little changed and indeed, little change was expected. It was well known that Herod had several sons (even though he had some of his male offspring killed on suspicion of having plotted against him), and so it was only a matter of time before one of these sons would seize the throne and continue the odious Herodian regime.

But, as we saw previously, the old king had a surprise in store for all of them. No doubt anticipating that his death would prompt an intense rivalry among his surviving sons for the crown, he proposed to his master, Emperor Augustus, that his kingdom be broken up along the familiar fault lines that had existed before the Hasmonean Restoration. In other words, Judea and Samaria would once again be separated from Galilee, whilst Galilee would be divorced from the territory to its immediate east, known as the Gaulanitis. This way, the pieces could be parceled out among his three principal sons—Archelaus, Antipas, and Philip—without the need for a long and bloody battle for the throne. The coastal territory of Ashdod was given to Herod's daughter Salome as a consolation prize of sorts. What this division also meant, however, was that none of these new rulers could claim Herod's traditional title of *basileus*—of "king." Their territories were simply too small to justify such.

None of these shocking developments were, as yet, known to Herod's sons. It was up to Augustus to review Herod's will and decide whether it was indeed in Rome's interest to carve up a territory that, from Rome's point of view, had done well as an integral kingdom. It had successfully suppressed any challenges to its rule and paid its tribute on time. That is why Herod's most senior heir, Archelaus, was completely oblivious to his late father's machinations and, after a proper mourning period had been observed, threw a huge party with his friends. Surrounded by music, women, and good wine, he feasted till dawn in Herod's Jerusalem palace, secure in the knowledge that the king's throne would soon be his. But he failed to see that underneath the surface, the nation was awash with discontent. Among the merchants and traders, the farmers and scribes, and the workers and artisans still toiling on the Second Temple complex, a revolt was brewing.

Oblivious to it all, Archelaus announced that he wanted to be more merciful and compassionate than his father, and rule as a man beloved by his people. That sparked a huge wave of appeals. Hundreds of men and women clamored for compensation for all the evil that had been done under Herod's regime. A good many, perhaps led by the Pharisees, demanded the immediate eviction of the high priest, appointed by Herod and universally regarded as one of his cronies. The people wanted a true high priest, one who would be genuinely concerned with justice based on the Torah. Alarmed by the breadth of discontent, Archelaus responded that until Augustus had confirmed him in office, he would not have the authority to make any changes. The rebellious mood then reached a climax during Passover of that year. The festival became a rallying point for demonstrations against the crimes of Herod's regime and the people's demand for change. Among the worshipers, says Josephus, were "a great number who had come from Galilee." One group of scholars and their students went as far as to organize a "sit-down" strike in the Temple. Well provisioned with food and water, they refused to budge until their demands had been met. In a panic, Archelaus did what most tyrants do when confronted with protest: he called in the army. As the infantry pushed into the Temple forecourt and horsemen thundered down the narrow streets of the Lower City, a bloodbath ensued. Those who ran from the forecourt were mercilessly cut down by the cavalry, with total casualties running as high as three thousand people. The survivors ran to the nearby hills.[2]

If Augustus had been in doubt about the wisdom of Herod's partition plan, the events in Jerusalem convinced him that no son of Herod's could be entrusted with ruling the kingdom. As Herod himself had anticipated, only a "divide and rule" policy could keep the ambitious Herodian brood in check. And so, while Archelaus sailed to Rome still blissfully unaware

| Map of the Herodian Kingdom after its partition as decreed in Herod's will.

of the news that awaited him there, Augustus dispatched a trusted diplomat named Sabinus in the opposite direction, to Jerusalem. There, Sabinus summoned all of Herod's senior officials and demanded that they give him a detailed accounting of the former king's properties and state income. Unbeknownst to Archelaus and his immediate family, the groundwork was being laid for a complete takeover of Judea, with Herod's son ruling as a mere puppet.

Meanwhile, the bloodbath in Jerusalem had sparked a revolt that rapidly spread throughout Judea, Samaria, and Galilee.

The whole country, now effectively without government, erupted in violence. Entire regiments of Herod's standing army disbanded and spread across the region, where they took to banditry. This is the moment that Judas, the son of Hezekiah, had been waiting for. Arguably, Judas' father was the same Hezekiah who had led a revolt in Galilee some thirty years earlier against Herod's ruinous policy of extracting funds for Cassius' army. Judas organized his own band of resistance fighters and set out to wage guerrilla warfare on anything and anyone associated with either the Herodian regime or the Romans: officials, landowners, and ordinary soldiers.[3]

We do not know to what extent the peasants of Galilee rallied to his cause, but given their suffering under Herod's regime, it would not come as a surprise to know that many of them threw their support behind Judas' rebellion. For years, their harvests and their lands had been sucked up by Jerusalem, there to further swell the coffers of Herod's elites. As the winds of freedom swept down from the hills, it would have been tempting to heed Judas' rallying cry and get payback from the rich landowners, their stewards, and their Roman overlords. What the rebels lacked, however, was weapons. To procure such arms, Judas and his rebels broke into an arsenal built by Herod in the city of Sepphoris, which lay some four miles distant from Nazareth, and took all the swords, bows, and javelins they could put their hands on. Inevitably, the region around Sepphoris now became a center of the revolt—and the target of the Roman retaliation that was sure to follow. Indeed, Governor Varus of Roman Syria, who held military authority over Herod's former kingdom, had already decided that a major response was needed. He promptly dispatched two legions from Antioch and fatefully invited many of Rome's vassal kings in the region to send auxiliary troops as well.

The request did not fall on deaf ears. For years, neighboring kingdoms such as Berytus and Nabataea—famous for its rock-hewn capital of Petra—had chafed under Herod's arrogant and belligerent rule. Now they could exact some revenge. Indeed, it was King Aretas of Nabataea and his Arab soldiers, who were closer to the main areas of guerrilla activity than the Roman legions, who plunged into Galilee with the objective of capturing Sepphoris and suppressing the Galilean rebels. Soon his forces killed, raped, and burned their way through Galilee toward Sepphoris. Directly in their path lay a small village called Nazareth.

How did this brutal conflict affect the young family of Joseph, Mary and Jesus? Seeing these Arab soldiers pillage the villages and fields in the area must have traumatized them. As Josephus tells us, "along their march nothing escaped them, but all places were full of fire and of slaughter." Perhaps Joseph's land was damaged or burned, along with other adjoining plots, dooming that year's harvest and plunging the family into hardship.

It was Jesus' first exposure to the vulnerability of the peasants under Roman occupation. Of course it is doubtful that the child, who was only one or two at the time, would have remembered, but the fear and destruction must have made an indelible impression on Joseph. It is possible that Joseph imparted the horror of these reprisals and the futility of opposing Rome to his son. Throughout his later years, Jesus would never advocate a confrontation with the Romans. Instead, he would urge his followers to "give Caesar what belongs to Caesar" (Mark 12:17). The Gospel of Luke even tells us that Jesus once agreed to heal the servant of a Gentile centurion stationed in Capernaum (Luke 7:1–10).

The Gospels do not refer to this rebellion at all, which is not surprising when we remember that all of the evangelists probably lived outside of Roman Palestine, and wrote at least some 70 years after these events. Mark is believed to have written his Gospel in Rome after the outbreak of another rebellion, the First Jewish War of 66 CE. Matthew and Luke wrote their Gospels in the two decades after Mark, for they borrow as much as 65 percent of Mark's Gospel in their story. It is not clear where Matthew and Luke lived, though some scholars have suggested either Asia Minor (today's Turkey) or Alexandria in Egypt. The Gospel of John was probably written near the end of the first century, quite possibly in Asia Minor as well. As a result, the evangelists relied heavily on oral traditions about Jesus that were circulating at that time, augmented by so-called "sayings documents"—records of what Jesus said and did. The Gospel of Thomas is such a sayings document (though its date is uncertain), as well as a putative source used by Matthew and Luke that scholars refer to as the Q document (for the German word *Quelle* or "source"), even though the original document no longer exists. We must therefore rely on the first-century Jewish historian Josephus, who carefully documented the political developments in Judea both before and after Herod's reign. Josephus is not particularly interested in the Jesus movement (even though he refers to Jesus in a much-debated paragraph), but his works have become an invaluable source for understanding the turbulent events that attended Jesus' youth, adolescence, and adulthood.

The only reference to Jesus as a young boy appears in the Gospel of Luke, when Jesus was twelve years old, just before his Bar Mitzvah. Mary and Joseph decided to take him to Jerusalem for the Passover festival, together with other pilgrims from nearby villages. But when they returned to Nazareth, they discovered that Jesus was not part of the group.

> When they did not find him, they returned to Jerusalem to search for him. After three days they found him in the Temple, sitting among the teachers, listening to them and asking them questions. And all who heard him were amazed at his understanding and his answers. (Luke 2:45–47)

The story is not found in any of the other Gospels, which suggests that we should look for an allegorical meaning that could have been apparent to Luke's audience. In ancient Judaism, as in most synagogues today, a boy or girl is believed to have reached maturity at age thirteen, when they become responsible for their actions. At that point they are expected to know the tenets of the Torah, the Jewish Law, which they demonstrate during their Bar or Bat Mizvah by reading from Scripture. In a sense, therefore, the story in Luke is meant to show that Jesus has a better understanding of the Torah than the scholars in the Temple. He is therefore qualified to adapt the Law to the unique conditions of his time, as he will do during his future ministry with his Kingdom of God program.

This raises an important question: was Jesus indeed educated, and if so, where would he have received his schooling? The Gospels clearly refer to Jesus as a rabbi, which means "teacher" (Mark 4:38) and suggests that Jesus must have had a deep familiarity with the Torah. The Mishnah indicates that by the third century CE, every town and village had a school, a *beit midrash*, attached to the local synagogue, where young boys were taught Scripture. Until recently, however, scholars dismissed this idea as a mere pious wish, since most villages could not afford to build and maintain a synagogue with its attendant teachers. What's more, these scholars argued, before 70 CE there was no point in having a synagogue in places like Galilee because most Jews, even poor ones, traveled to the Temple in Jerusalem for the three holy festivals. These festivals include Passover, celebrated in the month of Nisan (March/April); *Shavuot* or the Festival of Weeks, fifty days after the beginning of Passover; and *Succoth*, the Feast of Tabernacles, which came in the month of Tishri (September/October). In the Gospel of John, for example, there is an enigmatic reference to Jesus' brothers going to Jerusalem for Succoth and inviting Jesus to come along. Jesus refuses, saying that "my time has not yet come." But after his brothers have left, he decides to go after all, and travels "in secret" (John 7:2–10).

The prevailing theory about the absence of synagogues (and synagogue schools) in the time of Jesus was swept away by a dramatic discovery on the shores of the Sea of Galilee. Here, in the ancient town of Magdala, Israeli archaeologist Dina Avshalom-Gorni found the remains of what appears to be a synagogue. To everyone's surprise, the excavators located a coin *underneath* the floor of the synagogue, which was dated to 29 CE—exactly the time of Jesus. Up to this point, all synagogues found in Galilee dated to the third century CE or later. But the most exciting find was a room near the front of the synagogue, with a number of benches. This indicates that the room was a *beit midrash,* a school for young boys, exactly as described in the Mishnah two centuries later. It would therefore seem entirely plausible that an intelligent young boy like Jesus could have had his first encounter with Hebrew Scripture in a synagogue school such as the one in Magdala.

The beit midrash of the synagogue of Magdala, believed to date from the time of Jesus.

Then again, a *beit midrash* in itself does not provide the necessary education to become a rabbi. That took many years of study, either in a yeshiva or by having an individual tutor. As far as we know, there were no yeshivas of note in Galilee in Jesus' time. These were to be found in Judea, including two influential first-century academies led by Rabbi Hillel and Rabbi Shammai, respectively. In principle, it is not impossible that Jesus left for Judea to be educated there, but the evidence suggests otherwise. For that, we must once again turn to the political events that shaped so much of Jesus' youth.

In 6 CE, when Jesus was ten or eleven years old, word reached Emperor Augustus that Archelaus was mismanaging his territory of Judea and Samaria, and that it was on the verge of social and economic ruin. A delegation of Judean noblemen sailed to Rome, arguing that Archelaus was no longer fit to hold office, for "he had broken the commands of Caesar."[4] Augustus was in no mood to be indulgent. In the last four years, his grandsons and designated heirs, Lucius and Gaius Caesar—the former still in his late teens, the latter in his mid-twenties—had died under mysterious circumstances. The future of the Roman succession was in doubt, and the last thing Augustus needed was trouble in the provinces. Archelaus was summoned to Rome and summarily dismissed from his post as *ethnarch*, as "ruler of the people." He was banished to Vienne, a city on the left bank of the Rhône River in Gaul (modern France), and deprived of most of his money.

Archelaus' fall from grace would have fatal consequences for the history of ancient Israel. In a way it established the essential conditions that would ultimately lead to Jesus' death. For Augustus decided not to hand the territory of Judea and Samaria to Herod's *other* sons, Antipas and Philip, nor to return the sovereignty of this ancient land to its legitimate dynasty, the Hasmonean House. Instead, Augustus made the fateful decision to annex Judea, making it a subject province of Rome known as *Iudaea*, to be ruled by a Roman prefect reporting to the governor of Greater Roman Syria. Any pretense that Judea was still a self-governing nation was thus lost forever.

The decision infuriated Antipas, the *tetrarch* of Galilee and Perea. He had followed with keen interest how his brother was measured for the fall, and already saw himself as his logical successor, perhaps even with the title of *basileus* if Augustus decided to once again merge Galilee with Judea and Samaria. But the news that Judea was now to be governed as a Roman Crown province came as a shock. In his anger, Antipas decided that if he could not be king, then he would simply *act* as if he was one—by doing what his father Herod had done before him.

By building cities. Beautiful, well-planned *poleis* in sparkling marble, funded—naturally—by the heavy yoke of taxes that continued to vex the Galilean peasantry.

There was an obvious location that could benefit from such urban planning: the provincial capital of Sepphoris, large tracts of which had been burned and destroyed during the revolt ten years earlier. Located in the heart of Lower Galilee, almost equidistant from the Mediterranean and the Sea of Galilee, Sepphoris (or *Zippori* in Hebrew) had been a center of Galilee's provincial administration in the earliest days of the Roman conquest. And since the legions sent by the Roman governor Varus had done Antipas the favor of razing the old city to the ground, he could now build a true Greco-Roman city that, in Josephus' words, would become "the ornament of all Galilee."[5]

Who was going to build this new city? Why, the displaced and dispossessed farmers of the region, of course. A vast enterprise such as the construction of a city must have sucked resources and manpower from every corner of Lower Galilee. Scores of peasants would have been recruited to provide the muscle for hefting beams, hoisting smooth-hewn blocks of stone, or pounding slabs of pavement. It is inconceivable that the inhabitants of the tiny hamlet of Nazareth, in such close proximity to Sepphoris, would not have been affected. What's more, Joseph was a *tektōn*, a skilled worker, whose services would have been especially prized in the construction pits. And because in ancient times, sons always followed in the footsteps of their father, it is most likely that Jesus eventually wound up working in the rebuilding of Sepphoris as well. One reason is that, as the Gospels attest, Jesus' was not the only mouth Joseph had to feed. In the years since Jesus' birth, Mary had presented her husband with a steady succession of children, including four

brothers—James, Joses, Juda, and Simon (Mark 6:3). In addition, there were sisters; Mark does not tell us how many, since
apparently, girls did not rate as highly as men, but the plural
indicates that there were at least two.[6]

Consequently, I believe that sometime after Jesus reached
his thirteenth birthday, when a Jewish boy was considered old
enough to undergo his Bar Mitzvah, he joined his father in the
construction of Sepphoris, thus augmenting whatever meager
stipend Joseph was paid. True to Roman precedent, the new
city was equipped with a bathhouse and a basilica (a Roman
meeting hall used for civic functions) in addition to other,
multi-story buildings, all connected by paved streets such as the
marble pavement discovered in 2006.

Jesus' sojourn in Sepphoris is important for several reasons.
First of all, it is around this time that Joseph disappears from the
Gospel story, never to be heard from again. The death of a father
in ancient times was a significant event, for it inevitably made
the oldest son the new head of the household. You would therefore expect the Gospels to tell us when Joseph, a major character
in the Gospel of Matthew, passed from this world, leaving the
care of his family to his oldest son. But as we saw earlier, the
biographical details of Jesus' youth are scant if not non-existent,
since none of the evangelists lived in Galilee or could somehow
have been witnesses to these events. What they relied on was
oral tradition, and the fact that Jesus was pressed into service to
help build a Greco-Roman city did not serve that tradition, even
if the details of these years had been known, which is unlikely.

The second reason why Jesus' stay in Sepphoris is important is
that it may answer the question of where, and when, he received
his formal schooling in Scripture, beyond learning the Bible by
rote as he may have done in a *beit midrash*. All of the Gospels

suggest that Jesus was not only well versed in the Books of the Prophets but also highly articulate in debating the finer points of the Torah, the Jewish Law. In Luke, for example, Jesus reads from Isaiah in the synagogue of Nazareth, and all in attendance "wondered at the gracious words which proceeded out of his mouth" (Luke 7:22). That this was unusual for the son of a villager is attested by John, who notes that "the Jews marveled, saying, How does this man read letters, given that he has never had any formal learning?" (John 7:15).

The answer is that in ancient times, "formal learning" was not the only route to becoming a rabbi. One could be tutored in the Torah, and in time gain the necessary knowledge to be accorded the distinction of being a "teacher." Where in Galilee could such tutors be found? The answer is the administrative center of the provincial government—in Sepphoris, in other words. That is why, as I argued in my book *Young Jesus*, it is likely that as a young teenager without a father, he was taken under the wing of a kind teacher in Sepphoris. Indeed, the presence of ritual baths or *mikva'ot* indicates that the city had a sizable Jewish community as early as the beginning of the Hasmonean period. Furthermore, an analysis of an ancient "garbage dump," near the western summit of the site, by Billy Grantham of Troy State University, has identified a remarkable absence of pig bones, in contrast to such remains found near Gentile communities. Similarly, coins struck in Sepphoris in the first century CE scrupulously avoid the habitual portrait of the emperor. All these point to a Jewish observant population.

Given the need for educated officials and scribes in the Sepphoris administration, I also believe that the city had a large Pharisaic community. That argument is supported by the fact that archaeologists have recovered over a hundred fragments of

The theater of Sepphoris, originally built by Herod Antipas, was much expanded in the second century under Roman rule.

stone vessels in Sepphoris. Stone vessels, though expensive, were in great demand by pious and relatively affluent Jews—precisely the socioeconomic group among whom the Pharisees enjoyed great popularity—because liquids held in stone, rather than pottery, glass, or metal, could never become impure. The Pharisees, whom we will encounter throughout the stories of Jesus' ministry, were a pious group of religious laymen who rejected the idea that the only path to salvation led through the rite of animal sacrifice at the Temple.[7] They believed that, in contrast, a cleansing of mind and body could be realized by the meticulous application of Mosaic ritual purity on everything that a person touched, from the moment he got up to the time he went to sleep. The Pharisees are often depicted in the Gospels as people hopelessly obsessed with the minutiae of the Law. But in practice, they were a strong progressive element in Second Temple Judaism that continuously sought solutions for situations that the Mosaic Laws had never anticipated. Unlike the Sadducees, who considered the Torah a closed book, the Pharisees led the ongoing debate to apply the *principles* of the Law to the changing circumstance of Second Temple Judaism—a process known as the Oral Law.

Why would some of these Pharisees have taken the young Jesus under their wing? The answer may be that Jesus, who had recently lost his father, was an intelligent, inquisitive, and attentive young man. The Pharisees, moreover, were devoted to educating the young. Once invited into their midst, Jesus would have been intrigued by the Pharisaic idea that the Torah was *not* an immutable codex of human behavior: that Jews, in fact, had the freedom to interpret and debate the tenets of the Law; that God encouraged such exegesis and sent his divine Spirit to guide such deliberations, as the Spirit had guided prophets of days past; and that, lastly, the cumulative wisdom of these discussions, the Oral Law, could help Jews to better cope with the great social challenges of their time. All of these ideas, which are cornerstones of Pharisaic thought, would resonate strongly in Jesus' teachings. And this theory would explain why Jesus would become so familiar with Pharisaic tenets and customs, as countless episodes in the Gospels would later attest.

In 14 CE Emperor Augustus, who had ruled the Roman Empire for over forty years, passed away. An extraordinary period of peace in much of the known world—the celebrated *Pax Romana*—had seemingly come to an end, particularly because few people had ever heard of his successor, Augustus' stepson Tiberius. But in Galilee, the tetrarch Antipas greeted the news with joy. His relationship with Augustus had always been tense, but he had cultivated excellent connections with the Tiberius party. Emboldened by this relationship, Antipas made a momentous decision in or around 20 CE, when Jesus was twenty-four or twenty-five years old. He decided to shift his focus from the town of Sepphoris to the construction of a new city, located on the Sea of Galilee. To curry favor with the new emperor, he named it "Tiberias" in Tiberius' honor. This time, Antipas wanted to build a true Greco-Roman *polis*, unencumbered by Jewish sensitivities. He envisioned it as a splendid city with temples, a gymnasium, and bathhouses in the Hellenistic style. To that end he picked a spot close to several hot springs, now known as Hamat Tiberias, which had once been a Jewish cemetery. In Jewish eyes the site was therefore unclean; no observant Jew would want to work or live there. That was perfectly fine by Antipas, who wound up populating Tiberias with Gentiles from towns east of the Jordan, in the region known as the Decapolis (Greek for "Ten Cities").

The subsequent years, between 20 and 28 CE, might well be called the "lost years of Jesus." There is no evidence of what he may have done during this period. But I believe that this was a time when, released from working in Sepphoris, he began his practice as a young rabbi, serving the needs of the villages and hamlets of Lower Galilee, rather than living in his home town of Nazareth. One reason is that when he joined the movement of John the Baptist eight years later, he was already recognized as a rabbi (John 1:38). And the second reason is that, as we will see, Jesus felt a certain alienation from his family. In one of the oldest sayings traditions about Jesus, we hear him say wistfully, "Foxes have dens, and birds of the sky have nests, but the son of man has nowhere to lay his head."[8]

These journeys through Galilee brought him face to face with the terrible devastation wrought by the preceding four decades of economic exploitation. Villages once populated by freeholders were now poverty-stricken hamlets, crowded with families ravaged by hunger. Town and village squares were filled with unemployed men, waiting listlessly for an offer of a day's wages that might never come. The once-proud peasantry that had survived centuries of foreign occupation, that had withstood the encroachment of Gentile culture since the age of Alexander the Great, had finally succumbed. The Judean political elites, shielded by Roman law and Roman arms, had succeeded in grinding the Galilean peasants into submission, taxing them into debt, and then converting that debt into land appropriation. The ancient social fabric of Galilee was torn beyond recognition. It would have made Jesus angry and desperate to remedy their suffering.

One major outcome of that suffering was the rise of chronic disease and disabilities, largely as the result of the lack of proper nutrition during infancy. The Gospels are filled with the blind, the deaf, the lame, and those affected by other diseases, but few, if any, modern authors have ever tried to come to terms with the reason for these conditions. Traditionally, as we have seen, the subsistence farmers of Galilee had been able to feed their families with a fairly balanced diet of starch, vegetables, and fruit. Modern medical science tells us that a healthy and active child between four and eight years old needs to take in between 1,500 to 2,000 calories per day, including 20 to 30 percent proteins, 45 to 65 percent carbohydrates, and 25 to 35 percent fats, as well as 800 milligrams of calcium and 1200 milligrams of sodium.[9] While such modern concepts of nutrition were of course wholly unknown in Jesus' time, farmers may have had an intuitive sense of the need for such a balanced diet. Even in Rome, as Peter Garnsey has argued, the poor could usually supplement their diet with a modicum of cheap legumes (cabbage, leeks, beets, and onions) as well as wine, olive oil, and low-quality fish.[10] But when they lost their land, the Galilean peasantry also lost the ability to provide their families with balanced nutrition.

The idea that wholesale malnutrition during the regime of King Herod was responsible for the outbreak of chronic disease and disability is borne out by modern studies of the World Health Organization. In 2020, they showed that of all children under the age of five in the developing world, 159 million are stunted (low height for age), 50 million are wasted (low weight for height), and 167 million are underweight (low weight for age).[11] All of these conditions are invariably the result of a poor diet or malnutrition. In 1995 alone, 6.3 million of the 11.6 million deaths among children aged under five years were directly the result of malnutrition.[12] Vitamin A deficiency in particular would have inevitably led to eye disease, which is still common in developing countries today. A 1998 study in Latin America concluded that no less than 25 percent of children under the age of five in this region suffered from some form of vitamin A deficiency, with eye lesions and irreversible blindness being the most common manifestations. In rural areas, the incidence was as high as 41 percent.[13] In addition, a lack of vitamin C can also have severe consequences. One condition is known as osteomalacia, a bone disease that can have a devastating impact on pregnant and lactating women whose condition is aggravated by the loss of calcium inherent in pregnancy and breast feeding. It can also inhibit the formation of healthy bones in young children, in essence crippling them.[14]

The rapid deterioration of the peasant diet before and during the time of Jesus has been vividly illustrated by a detailed study of ancient fecal matter, preserved in household "toilets" excavated in areas of human habitation. In one study, paleoanthropologist Jane Cahill found evidence of a healthy diet of fruits and vegetables from specimens dating *before* the Roman occupation. Later archaeological finds, however, reveal not only a far less balanced diet, but also a dramatic increase in parasites and infectious agents. This malnutrition, in turn, weakened the human immune system, leading to an outbreak of disease on an unprecedented scale.[15]

We are so familiar with the stories of the blind, the crippled, the lame, and other disabled people in the Gospels that we unconsciously accept these conditions as a fact of life in ancient Galilee. But there is every reason to believe that the theme of illness and disease in the Gospels is so pronounced *precisely because it was so unprecedented.* For centuries, Galilean villages had been among the best-fed communities in the Middle East because of this region's fertility. Now, in the span of one generation, these same villages had succumbed to disease on an epidemic scale.

But what could Jesus do for these unfortunate people? He was a poor man himself; he had no money, no land, nor any food to give. He was undoubtedly a young man of great kindness and intelligence, but beyond that, what tangible comfort could he offer?

The answer is clearly attested in the Gospel literature. Jesus *did* have something special and something tangible to give. It was precisely this unique talent that may have motivated him to move among the poorest of the poor, knowing that he had something concrete to offer, something that could improve their lot in a significant way. For Jesus had discovered that he had the ability to heal.

As we will see in a later chapter, that is why the healing miracles play such a pivotal part in Jesus' ministry, and why reports of his healing ability spread through Galilee like wildfire, producing the multitudes who came from all over the region to see him. The health of the Galilean people became a paramount concern for Jesus—something that those who in our modern day want to deny access to health insurance to others should bear in mind. Matthew puts it best when he writes that "when [Jesus] saw the multitudes, he was moved with compassion for them, because they were harassed and helpless, like sheep without a shepherd" (Matthew 9:36).

The impetus for that ministry came in 28 CE. In that year, a shocking event in Jerusalem roiled the region and prompted many young men and women to flock to the leading dissident of their day—a man whom Josephus called "John the Baptizer."

| 3 |

ALONG THE BANKS OF
THE JORDAN

Every government that suppresses its people is bound to produce dissidents—people who raise their voice in protest at great risk to their personal wellbeing. In our age, we can see the valorous actions of dissidents on an almost daily basis—in places like Russia, China, Iran, Afghanistan and other nations that deprive their people of the right to speak their mind.

The Hebrew Bible is full of stories of such people. That is surprising, because the documents from other nations in this era do not tend to focus on those who denounce the unjust policies of their rulers. Instead, Greco-Roman stories are mostly about heroes who, favored by the gods, combat impossible odds to triumph in the end. The Hebrew Bible, however, reserves a very special place for those who stand up to their kings (or queens) whenever they stray from the path and purpose that God has given them. The Bible refers to those people as prophets, and not all of them are men. One famous prophetess, Deborah, rose up against the oppression of the Canaanites who deprived the Israelite tribes from access to the fertile plains and water sources of the Jezreel Valley. Of course, she realized that her tribe alone could not defeat the enemy. She therefore organized a *levée en masse* among all the Hebrews, and many tribes rallied to her cause. Under her leadership and that of her commander Barak, the Israelites rode out and defeated the 900 chariots led by the Canaanite general Sisera (Judges 5:3).

Not all biblical prophets were antagonists. Samuel was instrumental in the creation of a supreme commander over all the tribes in their struggle with the Philistines; this commander became Israel's first king, named Saul. Other prophets served as councilors to the courts of Judah or the Northern Kingdom, even though their council was not always welcome. But some had the courage to stand up and denounce the king when, in their eyes, the monarch acted against the will of God.

The prophet Ahijah, for example, was so incensed by the pagan worship that was raging at the court of King Solomon that he encouraged one of Solomon's ministers, Jeroboam, to plot Solomon's overthrow (1 Kings 11:4). It was the same cultivation of pagan practices that prompted the prophet Elijah to loudly denounce the rule of King Ahab and his Phoenician wife, Queen Jezebel (1 Kings 17:1). Similarly, the prophet Amos attacked the growing injustice in the Northern Kingdom because of the aggregation of land by rich landowners at the expense of local farmers (Amos 2:4–6). The prophet Micah, too, fulminated against the growing social ills in neighboring Judah (Micah 1:1).

In that sense, John the Baptist merely followed in the footsteps of so many prophets before him when he railed against the exploitation of the poor by the elites of Judea. According to Josephus, John the Baptist was a major dissident of his time who denounced the corruption of Jewish society and urged repentance. John "was a good man," Josephus says, "who exhorted the Jews to exercise virtue, both in terms of righteousness toward one another and piety toward God, and so come to baptism." John's message must have been successful, for Josephus claims that "crowds flocked to him, and they were greatly moved by his words." Mark's Gospel agrees that "people from the whole Judean countryside and all the people of Jerusalem were going out to him," and were "baptized by him in the river Jordan, confessing their sins" (Mark 1:5). Matthew even depicts John as a latter-day Elijah, whom the Book of Kings described as "a hairy man, with a leather belt around his waist" (Matthew 3:4; 2 Kings 1:8).

It is not difficult to understand the Baptizer's appeal. The nation of Judea was morally adrift and increasingly smitten with the sensuous culture of Rome. That is why John preached that a great cataclysm was on the horizon, a deluge more terrible than anything Israel had witnessed in its thousand-year history. Jews, said John, should make a total break with their sinful living and do so with the symbolic act of an all-cleansing submersion in water. By espousing these ideas, John tapped into a number of apocalyptic currents that had been steadily building over the previous two centuries. Scholars refer to these ideas as eschatological visions—prophecies, in short, about a catastrophic change in the near future that would end the world as we know it and leave only the righteous untouched. The Intertestamental Writings—books written by Jewish authors in the era between the Old and New Testaments—are full of apocalyptic visions, a genre rarely seen in earlier times. One such book is the Psalms of Solomon, written (despite its title) in the first century BCE, with its urgent desire for a "cleansing" of the nation by the firm hand of the Messiah: "May God cleanse Israel against the day of mercy and blessing, against the day of choice when He brings back His anointed (*Mashiach*). Blessed shall be they that live in those days, for they shall see the goodness of the Lord which He shall perform for the generation that is to come, under the chastening rod of the Lord's anointed, in the fear of his God, in the spirit of wisdom and righteousness and strength."[1] That language has a parallel in John's warning that the Messiah's "winnowing fork is in his hand, to clear his threshing floor . . . but the chaff he will burn with unquenchable fire" (Luke 3:17).

Knowing that he was treading a fine line between tolerated preaching and dangerous dissent, John was not operating in Judea proper. Instead, he had wisely established his base in Bethany-across-the-Jordan, in the territory of Perea. By a quirk of fate, Perea was ruled by Herod Antipas in his faraway palace in Sepphoris, rather than the Roman prefect in Judea.

What prompted Jesus to abandon his work as a rabbi in Galilee and to join the movement of John the Baptist is not clear. Luke, assuming the role of a Greek historian, places this moment "in the fifteenth year of the reign of Emperor Tiberius, when Pontius Pilate was governor of Judea, and Herod [Antipas] was ruler of Galilee" (Luke 3:1). The fifteenth year of Tiberius' reign equates to 28 CE, but Luke does not explain the significance of this specific date. Josephus, on the other hand, gives us a full report of what was happening in that volatile year of 28 CE.

For some time now, the new Roman prefect, Pontius Pilate, had been wondering how to derive a profit from his appointment to this hot and dusty land with its restive population. Alas, there was not a lot of commercial opportunity in Judea.

Bethany-on-the-Jordan, in today's Kingdom of Jordan, is believed to be the place where John the Baptist gathered his disciples.

Much of the agricultural production in the region was based in the tetrarchy of Galilee, outside of Pilate's jurisdiction. On top of that, the Judean economy was still recovering from the excess of Herod's building program some twenty years earlier. There were therefore hardly any liquid funds in the country—with one exception: the Temple treasury, known as the *korban* (a word synonymous with "gift" or "sacrifice"). This treasury was located in the Court of the Women of the Jerusalem sanctuary. It consisted of thirteen chests with tapering tops (*shoparoth*), akin to the shape of a trumpet—which is what the chests are called in the Talmud—to receive the donations and tithes from Jews throughout the land and the Diaspora beyond.[2] And so it is not surprising that Pilate would focus on this treasury, simply because it was the single largest concentration of capital in his realm.

The problem was how he could get his hands on it. Then Pilate hit upon an idea. He had observed that the Sadducee priests were scrupulous about taking their ablutions in special *mikva'ot,* ritual baths, built in their homes, which had to fed by running water. Obtaining such water in Jerusalem, in the heart of a dry, desert-like region, was a constant challenge; Herod had built a channel from Solomon's Pools to the Upper City of Jerusalem, but this conduit was wholly inadequate.

In response, Pilate proposed that he would build that great Roman invention, the aqueduct, which would carry fresh water from the mountains to the city and beyond. Who would fund this noble venture? Why, the Temple treasury, of course. After all, the priests were the ones who stood to benefit most from this rich new supply of fresh water. And so it came to pass. As Pilate had expected, the high priest Caiaphas proved to be amenable, and Pilate helped himself to the building funds. Construction was begun. But inevitably, the source of funding became known. The Judeans rose in uproar. Tens of thousands of protestors jammed into the Temple forecourt, denouncing the blatant theft of their hard-earned and sacred donations by the godless Romans. But Pilate was prepared. His soldiers infiltrated the crowds and upon a sign from Pilate, raised their swords. "They killed not only those that had participated in the demonstration," says Josephus, "but even innocent bystanders who had nothing to do with it." Luke's Gospel says that two years later, during his ministry, Jesus would actually meet some of the victims who had witnessed the great Temple Massacre: "There were some present who told him about the Galileans whose blood Pilate had mingled with their sacrifices" (Luke 13:1).

I believe it is possible that this shocking event was a catalyst for many young men and women to gravitate to this prominent figure in the desert, Jesus among them. For Jesus, too, was in search of a role model, a teacher, who could guide him into the next and pivotal phase of his life. In fact, Jesus' sojourn with John the Baptist could be seen as the third stage in his intellectual development. The first stage, as we have seen, was his education in the Torah, arguably by Pharisees. The second stage was his work among the rural villages of Galilee as a young rabbi, possibly guided by the writings of the eighth- and seventh-century BCE prophets, specifically Amos, Micah, and Jeremiah. The sojourn with John would complete Jesus' intellectual journey as he absorbed John's ideology as well as his unique brand of leadership.

Of course, we know very little about John's actual teaching. What we do know is gleaned from either the Gospels or the writings of Josephus. Based on these sources, we know that John had an urgent eschatological vision of Israel, and that he spoke of one "who comes after me" (John 1:15). This was arguably an agent of God's wrath, which had been kindled by the social injustice in the land of Israel. That is the thrust of John's teachings in the Gospel of Luke, where he exhorts his listeners to share their clothes and their food. The same segment also has John berating the "publicans," the tax collectors, to "collect no more than the amount prescribed to you." By the same token, soldiers are warned not to "extort money from anyone by threats or false accusation, and [to] be satisfied with your wages"—implying that such extortion was a common practice at the time (Luke 3:10–14). John delivered his sermons with a fiery, down-to-earth and often violent rhetoric, using simple metaphors—such as the winnowing fork, the ax, and the burning fire—that most Judeans would understand. Once, a group of newly arrived, well-meaning followers was promptly greeted as "a brood of vipers." John's calculated attack on the smug self-confidence of his contemporaries was meant to shake the listener from his complacency and force him to reassess his values and assumptions. John's clever use of immersion in the waters of the Jordan gave these people a tangible instrument of personal empowerment, of individual transformation.

It is this quality that must have resonated with Jesus. In the Baptist, Jesus had an opportunity to observe a bona fide charismatic leader up close and personal. It was as if Elijah, Jeremiah, or Isaiah had been beamed down from heaven for Jesus to witness in the flesh. This notion was quite real. In Matthew, Jesus speaks of John as the "Elijah who is to come" (Matthew 11:14). Significantly, the New Testament portrays John as a man dressed in a tunic of camel hair with a leather belt, eating locusts and wild honey, in a clear allusion to the prophet Elijah, who was similarly attired (Mark 1:6, 2 Kings 1:8). John was the Old Testament prophet personified, restored to life to denounce the unique circumstances of Jesus' time. In the years to come, Jesus would often pay homage to John as the great model of his movement. Was John a prophet? some asked. "Yes," Jesus replied in Luke, "and I tell you, more than a prophet." In fact, he continued, "no one among those born of women is greater than John" (Luke 7:26–28).

Another aspect of John that would make a profound impression on Jesus was his behavior toward his followers. Hebrew Bible prophets had rarely cultivated a following. Their activity was targeted on the members of the nation's elite, quite often the king himself. John's followers, by contrast, prayed, ate, and slept with him in the open desert. They went where he went. This unusual entourage gave John both social stature and ideological gravitas. The idea of a messianic movement being led by a rabbi or "teacher" is an idea that we also find in the community of Qumran, which kept and hid the famous Dead Sea Scrolls. According to the Damascus Document, the Qumran community was formed in the mid-second century BCE under the leadership of a "Teacher of Righteousness." It was this teacher, says one document, "to whom God has disclosed all the mysteries of the words of his servants the prophets."[3] In addition, the Teacher of Righteousness is presented not only as a prophet but also as an agent of salvation. By following his example, the people would find renewal of Israel's covenant of God. The parallel with Jesus' future ministry is obvious. Jesus, too, would be known as a rabbi (or "teacher"), likewise called by the spirit of God to prophesize and to bring salvation to the people of Israel.

The evangelists may have been aware of John's fame, but this celebrity posed a serious challenge. At the end of the day, who was more famous: John or Jesus? Josephus, who clearly has no preference for either figure, makes no bones about it. In Josephus' book *Antiquities of the Jews,* Jesus merits only one short (and highly controversial) paragraph, while the historian dedicates half a page to the works of John. In response, the evangelists make an effort to subordinate John's ministry to that of Jesus. In their view, John serves Jesus as his herald, rather than as his teacher. He is the Samuel who anoints Jesus as the Davidic Messiah in the Jordan River. And from these cool green waters rose a new man, dedicated to transforming the people of Galilee into the nation under God they had once been.

Alas, John's days were numbered. He had run afoul of Herod Antipas, the tetrarch of Galilee, by denouncing his second marriage to the wife of his half-brother Philip, a woman named Herodias.[4] As we saw, Perea—the region where John operated—had been granted to Antipas' tetrarchy, even though it was not contiguous with Antipas' home territory of Galilee. To complicate the matter of this marriage further, Herodias was also the daughter of another half-brother, Aristobulus (son of Herod the Great and Princess Mariamne). But Antipas persisted in pursuing Herodias for the oldest reason in the world: he was in love.

According to Matthew, John then accused Antipas of violating Covenant Law, saying that "it is not lawful for you to have your brother's wife," particularly if this wife had borne children to her first husband, as Herodias had evidently done (Mark 6:18). John based himself on the command in Leviticus that "you shall not uncover the nakedness of your brother's wife; it is your brother's nakedness" (Leviticus 18:16). This attack on the legitimacy of the marriage to Herodias then set into motion the train of events that would ultimately lead to the Baptist's death.

Josephus, however, has a different version of John's arrest. In his view, Antipas feared that John would be tempted to exploit the region's instability, since in his eyes John had the "power and inclination to raise a rebellion." Matthew agrees when he states that "[Antipas] feared the multitude, because they counted

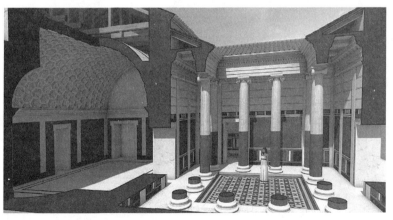

This reconstruction by the Hungarian Academy of Arts shows the interior of Herod Antipas' palace in Machaerus, where John was beheaded.

[John the Baptist] as a prophet" (Matthew 14:5). As Josephus writes, Antipas "thought it best, by putting [John] to death, to prevent any mischief he might cause, rather than get himself in difficulty by sparing a man who might make him regret it when it would be too late."[5] Josephus' interpretation of the events is valuable because it speaks volumes about the political atmosphere of the time—a time of growing tensions between the native Jewish population on the one hand, and the Romans and their collaborators on the other.

What is interesting about the case of John the Baptist is that Antipas moved against John without involving the seventy-one-member Jewish Council of the Great Sanhedrin. Though the Sanhedrin was based in Jerusalem, in Judean territory, it is believed that the Council had authority throughout Roman Palestine in religious matters, and John was one of the most charismatic religious figures of his time. This may explain why John was put to death in the desert fortress of Machaerus, far away from prying eyes, as Josephus tells us.

In the meantime, says the Gospel of John, a small number of the Baptist's followers crossed over to Jesus and named him their new teacher. Significantly, this group was composed of Galileans, including Simon Peter, his brother Andrew, and Philip, who were all from Bethsaida. After John was arrested, they packed what meager belongings they had and followed Jesus on the long journey north.

The years of preparation had come to an end. Jesus was ready to return to his native land and embark on his great campaign for the restoration of Israel.

| 4 |

JESUS LAUNCHES
HIS MINISTRY

Capernaum, located in the tetrarchy of Antipas west of the River Jordan, was the home town of Peter's wife and her family. Known as *Kfar Nahum* or "Nahum's village," it was a prosperous town because of its location, straddling the road from Damascus to Jerusalem, right on the border between Galilee and the Gaulanitis. It therefore had a tollbooth as well as a small military garrison, while its location on the Sea of Galilee made it a convenient base for shipping traffic across the entire lake. It was also known for its basalt industry, which was found nearby; most of the town's residences were, in fact, built with basalt stone.

Jesus decided to make this pleasant seaside town the launch platform for his Galilean campaign. It was here that he chose to reveal himself as a teacher in the mold of John. The actual place, says Mark, was the local synagogue. And so, "when the Sabbath came, [Jesus] entered the synagogue and taught." The towns-people were "astounded at his teaching, for he taught them *as one having authority,* and not as the scribes" (Mark 1:21–22). We can imagine their surprise: the young man from Nazareth, known for his charitable work among the poor, had suddenly become a rabbi who spoke expertly and confidently about Scripture.

To further underscore Jesus' authority, Mark relates how a man possessed by a "demon" appeared in the synagogue. Jesus rebuked the unclean spirit, and it left the man. The exorcism not only sealed Jesus' new role as a teacher, but also as a man with power over *demons*—henchmen of Satan. By exorcising evil spirits, Mark tells us, Jesus showed himself capable of taking on the great eschatological battle between the forces of good and evil.[1]

The news of the exorcism rapidly spread across the region, particularly because—as we have seen—chronic disease had become so endemic in Galilee. And so, says Luke, "as the sun was setting, all those who were sick with various kinds of dis-eases were brought to him; and he laid his hands on each of them and cured them." Others were likewise possessed by demons. They "also came out of many, shouting, "You are the Son of God!" (Luke 4:40–41). In ancient times, when people suffered from a chronic illness, they were believed to be pos-sessed by *daimónia* or demons. In Luke's view, because these demons are supernatural, they already recognize him as a son of God, the Jewish qualification of a Messiah, even when the people around him do not.

Now that his ministry was set in motion, Jesus was ready to expand his circle of disciples beyond the core of the Baptist's followers. In ancient times, it was customary for a pupil or *mathētés* to seek out a teacher and ask him if he was prepared to

The impressive limestone synagogue of Capernaum, which is now dated to the early fourth century.

accept him. But Jesus had another way of attracting disciples. He was going to *recruit* them. What's more, he knew where he could find them: among the fishermen of Capernaum. Mark describes how Jesus walked along the shore of the Sea of Galilee, where fishermen were busy cleaning and repairing their nets. There he found "James son of Zebedee and his brother John, who were in their boat mending the net." Jesus called to them, and immediately "they left their father Zebedee in the boat with the hired men and followed him" (Mark 1:19–20).

Jesus was in a hurry. He knew that he could not organize his campaign and make a significant impact in Lower Galilee all by himself. He needed a group of *talmidim,* of followers who could serve as the core support of his movement. Such followers would not only be able to propagate his *halakah,* his exegesis of Scripture, but also to assist him in arranging for food, shelter, and a place to speak. In sum, the followers that Jesus had in mind would not be students in the Platonic tradition, nor disciples in the Johannine mold, but *delegates,* empowered to assist the teacher and speak on his behalf. "Delegate" is, in fact, the translation of *shaliach,* which in the Gospels is translated as *apóstolos* or "apostle."

But why fishermen? In Antiquity, sages and wise men typically surrounded themselves with bright young pupils who were not yet married or vested in a given profession. These fishermen, on the other hand, were men like Simon Peter who had wives and families to support. For them, fishing would have been a full-time position, with little time to also serve as Jesus' emissaries. The answer may be that the dislocation of the peasantry from their ancestral lands had resulted in the growth of a vast proletariat without homes or means of support. Many of these men, both young and middle-aged, would have converged on the Sea of Galilee. Here, they reasoned, was still a harvest to be had, a harvest of fish. Consequently, the lake in Jesus' time must have been teeming with fishing boats both large and small. Inevitably, this vast increase in activity led to over-harvesting and the gradual depletion of the fish stocks. We find the evidence in the Gospel of Luke, in which a morose Simon Peter tells Jesus that they have "toiled all night long, and not caught anything." Jesus urges him to throw his nets one last time. And lo, Simon Peter and his crew bring in such a huge catch that their nets nearly break. Luke says that at that moment, "many ships from nearby" rushed to the scene to help and to get their share of this unexpected boon (Luke 5:4–7).

Jesus, however, wanted to recruit fishermen for a different reason: they typically had access to a boat, which they often leased as a cooperative. Luke confirms this when he refers to

"James and John, sons of Zebedee, who were partners (*koinōnoi*) with Simon" (Luke 5:10). These men may not all have been established, full-time fishermen but newly arrived workers "for-hire" or "freelance contractors" as we would call them today, with the freedom to move with Jesus from village to village. For that was Jesus' intended modus operandi: rather than waiting for people to come to him, as John the Baptist did, he would move across the region, often trying to visit several villages in a day. A boat gave him the means to do that.

Now equipped with a following of his own and the means to traverse the region, Jesus dedicated the remaining eighteen months of his life to propagating his great plan for social renewal in Galilee. This plan was a manifesto that Jesus himself referred to as "the Kingdom of God." With this manifesto, Jesus aimed for a grass-roots surge of renewal that would end the social and

The Galilee Boat, which was miraculously discovered along the shore of the Sea of Galilee in 1986, has since been dated to the early first century CE.

economic exploitation of the poor by the nation's elites and restore Israel as a nation governed by Yahweh.

Various scholars have pointed out that the term "Kingdom of God" is relatively unknown in the Hebrew Bible before the Second Temple period, and therefore could be construed as a concept original to Jesus—and, by extension, to Christianity. Indeed, in Christian theology the "Kingdom of God" would later become a program of universal salvation, available to all who agree to be baptized in the name of Jesus Christ. For Christians, the physical manifestation of the "Kingdom" is the *ekklesia,* the Church on earth, preparing the faithful for the heavenly Kingdom that awaits after death.

But even a cursory reading of the Hebrew Bible makes it clear that the idea of a "Kingdom of God" was a deeply rooted principle of post-Exilic Judaism, certainly in the growing apocalyptic yearning of the Late Second Temple period. From the very first, the twelve tribes who settled in the Promised Land believed themselves to be a nation, or a *kingdom,* of God. Unlike the Christian God, the God of Hebrew Scripture was always a political and historical force, actively steering Israel's future. Time and again, Yahweh would intervene to safeguard his people, whether to engineer their release from bondage, to plot their strategy of conquest, or to punish kings who were seduced by pagan heresy. The books of the Bible that scholars refer to as the Deuteronomistic history breathe the fundamental principle that while kings may come and go, God is the ultimate ruler of Israel's destiny, just as the land on which the settlers live—the Promised Land—is God's land. The "Kingdom of God" therefore is the physical manifestation of God's plan for Israel, as a community who cleave to the three principal tenets of Covenant Law: compassion, social justice, and faith in God.

The way Jesus saw it, this was the raison d'être of the Jewish commonwealth; without it, the nation had no moral compass, no manifest destiny. But now, the land had strayed far from the ideals of its original founding. One reason was the seductive influence of Hellenistic civilization, a culture rooted in pagan motifs. Another was the growing schism between rich and poor, accelerated by the economic exploitation by the Romans and their collaborationist elites. And throughout it all, the priest-hood remained indifferent to the plight of the poor, focusing instead on little else but the sacrificial operations at the Temple.

It had not always been that way. After the return from the Babylonian Exile, a priestly elite had risen to lead the restoration of Israel as a religious entity. Ezrah and Nehemiah had not only rallied the people behind the newly codified precepts of the Law; they had also urged social justice, actively protecting the people from the excess of economic growth. Once, during a severe famine, owners of small plots complained that they had to mortgage their fields and vineyards to buy grain and pay the Persian king's tax, thus allowing nobles and officials to confis-cate their mortgaged land. Some were even driven to sell their children into slavery. Nehemiah became very angry. "Restore to them, this very day, their fields, their vineyards, their olive orchards," Nehemiah demanded, and the oligarchs complied (Nehemiah 5:1–13).

Now compare this to the priesthood of the early first century. In Jesus' day, the chief priests had ossified into an aristocratic elite, oblivious to the massive social crisis in the land. They pre-ferred to preoccupy themselves with cultivating their prerogatives and control of the operations at the Temple. Talmudic literature shows that high priestly families such as the houses of Boethus, Phiabi, and Kathros were among the wealthiest in Roman Palestine, as was the house of Hanin, which had produced Annas and his son-in-law, the current high priest Caiaphas. All of these families used their position to amass fabulous fortunes, with which they built large mansions in Jerusalem's Upper City. A rabbinic sage known as Abba Saul ben Batnit, who lived in Jerusalem some ten years after Jesus' crucifixion, claimed that the high priests appointed their sons as treasurers of the Temple and ordered their servants to go out and beat debtors with their fists and staves.[2] Rather than serving as pastors to the nation, as shepherds of their sheep, these chief priests actively collaborated with the Roman occupation so as to keep their grip on the sacrificial and financial operations of the Temple. Not surprisingly, perhaps, at the outbreak of the First Jewish Revolt in 66 CE, the feared *Sicarii* or "dagger men" immediately moved to kill the high priest while sending many other wealthy citizens fleeing for their lives. In the end, all of the chief priests were unceremoniously put to the sword. Their homes, including the palatial mansions of former chief priests such as Annas and Caiaphas, were burned to the ground.[3]

Many Jews before Jesus had recognized the illegitimacy and moral corruption of the priesthood during the Late Second Temple period. Some, such as the Essenes, fled Jerusalem to places like Qumran, where they created their own idea of a Kingdom of God in the form of a monastic community. Others, notably the Pharisees, transferred the idea of the Kingdom of God to their homes, by observing priestly conventions about purity and Sabbath observance in their own daily lives.

But Jesus' vision was radically different. Its purpose was to please God with one's heart and to share responsibility for the welfare of one's fellow man. "Why do you see the speck in your neighbor's eye, but do not notice the log in your own eye?" he thunders in one of his speeches (Matthew 7:3). "Shame on you, scribes and Pharisees," he says elsewhere, speaking as one who has observed Pharisaic customs up close: "for you tithe mint, dill, and cumin, but you neglect the weightier matters of the law: justice and mercy and faith" (Matthew 23:23). At times it seems Jesus is harking back to Jeremiah, who had also spoken of God's kingly reign shepherding the poor and downtrodden of Israel. "Behold," Jeremiah said, "if you truly amend your ways, if you truly act justly with one another, if you do not oppress the alien, the orphan, and the widow, or shed innocent blood," then God "would dwell in this land" (Jeremiah 7:1–7). A more succinct summary of Jesus' Kingdom program can scarcely be found.

No matter where we turn in the Gospels, the Kingdom of God is the very core of Jesus' teachings—in his parables, in his conversations with his followers, and most importantly, in the Sermon of the Mount. Nowhere do we find a more detailed explanation of Jesus' Kingdom of God doctrine than in his speech, which tradition has located on a lovely hill on the northern shore of the Sea of Galilee, close to Tabgha, believed to be the place of the miraculous multiplication of loaves and fishes. The hill offers a gorgeous view of the Sea of Galilee, and more importantly, provided a natural amphitheater that could amplify his voice for the hundreds, or perhaps thousands, of men, women, and children who came to listen to his words.

Of course, there are differences between Luke's and Matthew's versions of this sermon, as happens when things are transmitted by word of mouth. For example, Matthew's version is more legalistic, with strict rules and regulations, almost as if Jesus were engaged in a Pharisaic debate. In Luke, Jesus' sermon is filled with compassion and hope. Here, for the first time, we hear Jesus speak at length, in his own words.

Its stirring prologue is structured around eight blessings, known as the Beatitudes, each of which begins with the Greek expression *Makarioi*, "Blessed (are) . . ." In Matthew's Gospel, Jesus' sermon opens as follows:

> Blessed are the poor in spirit, for theirs is the kingdom of heaven.
> Blessed are those who mourn, for they will be comforted.
> Blessed are the meek, for they will inherit the earth.
> Blessed are those who hunger and thirst for righteousness, for they will be filled. (Matthew 5:3–6)

From these verses it is obvious that Jesus engages his audience very differently than his former teacher, John the Baptist. Whereas John deliberately tried to provoke his audience, Jesus reaches out to his listeners with empathy, by acknowledging their suffering. In Matthew's version, the sermon then develops into a set of *mitzvot,* a series of legal precepts that go well beyond the ethical parameters of the Torah. In fact, they appear to dismiss the principle of ancient Judaism that Jews can atone for their digressions with animal sacrifice. "If you remember that your brother or sister has something against you," Jesus says, "leave your gift there before the altar and go; first be reconciled to your brother and sister, and then come and offer your gift " (Matthew 5:21–24).

Luke's version of the Sermon approaches the Kingdom vision from a different perspective. In his Gospel, the emphasis is less on enforcing moral precepts than on the pursuit of social justice.

Blessed are you who are poor, for yours is the kingdom of
God.
Blessed are you who are hungry now, for you will be filled.
Blessed are you who weep now, for you will laugh.
Blessed are you when people hate you, and when they exclude
you, revile you, and defame you on account of the Son of
Man. (Luke 6:20–22)

As in the Gospel of Matthew, Jesus uses the paradox, a favored
motif in the Middle East, to shock his audience out of their
complacency. Why would anyone think that those who are
hungry and malnourished are happy and blessed? But by doing
so, Jesus not only identifies with the suffering of his listeners; he
also gives them hope by affirming their dignity and promising
their deliverance in the Kingdom.

And then, right after these soothing words, Luke's sermon
goes on the attack against those who are responsible for the
exploitation of the poor in Galilee. "Woe to you who are rich,"
says Jesus, "for you have received your compensation. Woe to you
who are full now, for you will be hungry. Woe to you who are
laughing now, for you will mourn and weep" (Luke 6:24–25).

To accomplish a society in which all these indignities would
be resolved through the overarching power of *agápē,* of selfless love, would become the singular focus of Jesus' ministry.
Whereas most of Jesus' contemporaries looked for an outside
intervention, a great cataclysm or a violent regime change to
establish the reign of God, Jesus made his case by expressing
his belief in people power. His kingdom concept was not a new
Davidic polity but a new way in which society would behave
toward one another. What Jesus envisioned was a new social
covenant whereby Jews pledged to return to the quintessential

virtues of the Law: compassion toward one another; justice toward the poor and the weak; and love and faith in God. Note, for example, that Jesus never performs a sacrifice, the principal redemptive practice of Second Temple Judaism. In this, Jesus may have remembered prophets such as Hosea, who said, "I desire mercy rather than sacrifice, and the knowledge of God rather than burnt offerings" (Hosea 6:6).

This is the message that Jesus brought to his core constituency, the poor of Galilee, and they cleaved to it with all their hearts. At the same time, they were probably wondering: *when?* When would this great Kingdom of God come about? The answer to this difficult question is uniquely Jesus'. The practical vehicle for implementing the Kingdom was his inspired idea, and his alone, for it is found nowhere else in the Hebrew Bible. Perhaps its purest expression can be found in the Gospel of Thomas. In it, Jesus says that "[the Kingdom of God] will not come by waiting for it. It will not be a matter of saying

The Church of the Beatitudes, built in 1937, is traditionally believed to be the place where Jesus delivered his Sermon on the Mount.

'Here it is' or 'There it is'" (Thomas 13). In Luke, Jesus puts it even more strongly: "The kingdom of God is not coming with things that can be observed" (Luke 17:20). What is that supposed to mean? If you can't tell if or when it comes, how can you know that the Kingdom of God has arrived? But Jesus explains: "For in fact, the kingdom of God is *among you*" (my italics). We the people, says Jesus, have the power to take destiny in our own hands, to join together to rid our villages and towns of the greed, the injustice, and the disease that has plunged Galilee into despondency. We can experience and live the Kingdom today—by acts of compassion toward our fellow human beings and an obedient love of God.

We are, perhaps, reminded of the words of Mohandas Gandhi, who urged his followers to "be the change you want to see." For Jesus, the Kingdom of God was not a political institution, but a state of grace, in anticipation of the great Kingdom of Heaven after death. As Martin Buber put it: "the Kingdom . . . is no other-worldly consolation, no vague heavenly bliss. It is the perfect life of man with man."[4]

Building a better society is not a zero-sum game, Jesus says. It's not about me winning and you losing. It's about us, together, trying to find common ground, and to make our world a better place for everyone, rich or poor, Black or white—and not just for those who think the same way we do. That's what being a Christian, *of walking with Jesus*, is all about.

To underscore the validity of this vision, Jesus used his healing ability to full effect. Not only did his natural talent for healing legitimize him as a man favored by God; each act of healing was also a tangible example of the restorative power of a community embracing solidarity and compassion—a vivid example of the Kingdom of God in action. As we saw, disease played an important role in the ancient world, and also in the Bible. Some, such as skin disease, made a person ritually impure (Leviticus 13:8). That meant that such patients could be ostracized from their community, further adding to their misery. Fear of illness was always foremost on people's minds in ancient times, because there were few defenses against contagious or chronic diseases. Perhaps for this reason, the Bible shows that God—as well as those touched by his divine spirit, such as the prophets—often had the power to heal. "I will not bring upon you any of the diseases that I brought upon the Egyptians; for I am the Lord who heals you," says God in Exodus (Exodus 15:26). The Prophet Elijah, too, demonstrated his miraculous powers when he breathed life into a widow's son who had died (1 Kings 17:22). His protégé, the Prophet Elisha, cured Naaman, a commander of the Syrian army, of leprosy (2 Kings 5:14). One Psalm exhorts its listeners to praise the Lord, "who forgives all your iniquities, who heals all your diseases" (Psalm 103:2–3).

The Gospels tell us that this was a major factor in Jesus' rapidly growing fame in Galilee and beyond. "And they brought to him all the sick," says Matthew, "those who were afflicted with various diseases and pains, demoniacs, epileptics, and paralytics" (Matthew 4:24). Indeed, says Mark, he cured so many people that "all who had diseases pressed upon him to touch him" (Mark 3:9–10). Eventually, says Luke, rumors of his healing powers spread far and wide, so that "a great multitude of people from all Judea, Jerusalem, and the coast of Tyre and Sidon" converged "to hear him and to be healed of their diseases" (Luke 6:17–18).

In biblical times, birth defects and chronic diseases were often believed to have a supernatural origin. Many illnesses or disabilities were regarded as God's punishment for sins—either by the patient or by his parents. If a child was born blind or deaf, for example, it was commonly believed to be the will of God as punishment for the sins of his or her parents. Man was formed in the image of God, says Genesis; it therefore followed that if a baby was malformed at birth, the baby must have been conceived in sin or doomed to suffer the punishment for his parents' transgressions. This is why, when Jesus' followers encountered a man who has been blind from birth, they asked Jesus, "Rabbi, who sinned, this man or his parents, that he was born blind?" (John 9:1–2). Jesus resolutely rejected such perceptions of the ill. "Neither this man nor his parents sinned," Jesus states emphatically in the Gospel of John. "He was *born* blind so that God's works might be revealed in him" (John 9:3).

The great appeal of miracle healers such as Jesus lay in the fact that medicine stood at its infancy, and medical services, such as they were, only existed in major cities, far removed from ancient Israel. Much of what the Romans believed or practiced about medicine was rooted in the work of Greek physicians such as Hippocrates, Herophilus, and Erasistratus, and further developed by Roman practitioners such as the famous Aelius Galenus or Galen. The physician Soranus published a series of books on gynecology in the second century, which includes some precepts that are still applicable today. But many of these regimens were of practical use only for common and survivable afflictions, such as superficial inflammations, skin burns, breach birth, excessive menstrual flow, or bowel ailments. Against the chronic diseases described in the Bible, ancient medicine was largely powerless— even if it had been available in Galilee, which was most certainly not the case.

| *A Greek physician with a young patient in a second-century Roman relief.*

As a result, medical doctors had a rather poor reputation in the ancient world. Their spotty record of success is vividly illustrated by the case of a woman who suffered from blood flow for twelve years. "She had endured much under many physicians, and had spent all that she had," Mark notes sorrowfully, "and she was no better, but rather grew worse" (Mark 5:26). Jesus was aware of the general antipathy against doctors and their bizarre treatments. "Doctor, cure yourself!" he says mockingly in the Gospel of Luke, perhaps quoting from a popular proverb (Luke 4:23). This may help us to understand why people flocked in such numbers to witness the healings and exorcisms that Jesus was reputably capable of. Parents of sick children, such as "one of the leaders of the synagogue named Jairus" were desperate to find a remedy, *any* remedy, to alleviate the suffering or even death of their loved ones (Mark 5:22; Luke 8:41).

For Jesus, his healing ability was vivid proof that the Kingdom of God could become a tangible reality, if only people abandoned their selfish ways and actively worked together to build a more just and compassionate society. But the hard part was to convince the actual agents of corruption: the soldiers, the tax collectors, the landowners, and other elites who continued to exploit the Galilean masses for their personal gain. That is why we see him, time and again, sitting down for dinner with tax collectors and other undesirables, much to the dismay of some. The Pharisees were horrified, for there was no telling whether the food was kosher or whether the cups and plates were ritually pure.[5] But the fellowship of the meal was an essential ingredient of Jesus' strategy to bring about change—particularly by breaking bread with those who had the power to lift the poor and alleviate their suffering. And to drive that message home, Jesus urged his table fellows to share their blessings with others. "When you give a banquet," Jesus said, "invite the poor, the crippled, the lame, and the blind"—a constituency that Jesus knew well (Luke 14:12–13). People had to understand that social division would no longer be tolerated in the Kingdom of God society; favoritism or preferential treatment at the expense of others would no longer exist.

During another banquet, held at a wedding, Jesus watched as his companions jockeyed for the seats of honor. In the Jewish tradition, guests were seated in order of seniority, starting from the left side of the table. Jesus corrected them, saying, "When you are invited, sit down at the lowest place, so that when your host comes, he may say to you, 'Friend, move up higher.' For all those who exalt themselves will be humbled, and those who humble themselves will be exalted" (Luke 14:7–11).[6]

What did such a meal look like? Traditionally, the average Galilean had lived on a diet of bread, dates, date honey and figs, and only at very special occasions, such as a wedding or the birth of a child, a piece of meat. Sheep, goats, and fattened calves were the preferred sources of meat, particularly for affluent households (Amos 6:4). In one of Jesus' parables, the return of a prodigal son is the occasion for the slaughter of a fatted calf (Luke 15:30). Remnants of meat were often used to make stews. In Jewish observant households, the kosher laws of the Torah restricted the types of animal meats that could be eaten. Only cattle and game that have "cloven hooves" and "chew the cud"—such as bulls, cows, sheep, lambs, and goats—could be used for consumption. By contrast, swine, badgers, hares, and camels, which do not meet these criteria, were not considered kosher and could therefore not be consumed (Leviticus 11:4–8). Another source of meat was fowl, such as turtledoves, quail, pigeon, or goose (1 Kings 4:23). Chickens only became domesticated in this region during the late Persian and Roman periods (Matthew 23:37). Furthermore, a mother and her offspring of any kosher species could never be slaughtered on the same day. All kosher animals had to be slaughtered by a *schochet,* a qualified ritual slaughterer, to avoid unnecessary pain for the animal and ensure near-instantaneous death.

Because the Torah prohibits the possibility of a young animal being cooked in the milk of its mother, dairy and meat products were always served separately; they could never be eaten together at the same table, as is still observed in kosher families

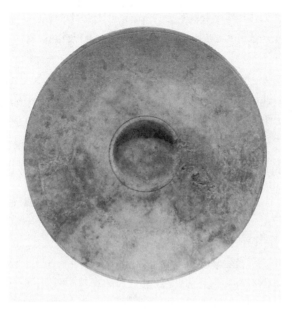

A first-century terracotta dish, with a depression in its center for sauce.

today. That means that after eating a portion of meat, one was expected to wait several hours before eating any dairy products. These restrictions did not apply to fish, though only fish with fins and scales—such as herring, salmon, tuna, sardines, or St. Peter's fish—could be consumed, whereas bottom-feeding fish could not (Leviticus 11:9–12). Coriander *(gad),* cumin *(kammon),* and dill *(qesah)* were important seasonings, as was salt *(melah)* (Job 6:6). For dessert, people who were privileged with access to such delicacies munched on honey cakes, raisins, figs, cakes of figs, or fruits in season (1 Samuel 30:12).

Beverages included water, milk (from cows, goats, or sheep), or wine. Wine, the fermented juice of crushed grapes, was consumed by almost everyone who could afford it (Judges 19:19; 1 Samuel 16:20; John 2:3). Originally, wine was usually uncut

(Isaiah 1:22), but in Jesus' day people had begun to mix wine with water, largely under the influence of Hellenistic customs.

And so, for eighteen months, Jesus traveled tirelessly through the hills and fields of Galilee, carrying the message of the Kingdom of God to the villages and towns. Mark puts it most succinctly: "Jesus came into Galilee, preaching the Gospel of the kingdom of God, and saying, 'the time is fulfilled, and the kingdom of God is at hand'" (Mark 1:14–15).

His guiding theme remained the words of Isaiah, which Luke has him read in the village assembly of Nazareth: "The Spirit of the Lord is upon me, for he has anointed me to bring good news to the poor. He has sent me to proclaim release to the captives and recovery of sight to the blind, to let the oppressed go free, to proclaim the year of the Lord's favor" (Luke 4:18). The "good news" (*euangelion* in Greek, translated in English as "goodspell" or "Gospel") was rooted in Jesus' firm belief that he not only could but *would* succeed—that the villages and towns in the wake of his visits would hearken to his words and embrace God's new society of faith, justice, and compassion.

Unfortunately, the Apostles—uneducated fishermen and day laborers mostly—struggled to understand Jesus as he developed and elaborated his Kingdom of God program. Repeatedly, they asked their teacher to explain it. The same is true for his mostly illiterate audience. In response, Jesus felt the need to illustrate the abstract ideas he talked about with simple metaphorical stories, known as parables. At first glance, they are easy to understand. Most parables are inspired by common "genre" scenes taken from everyday life in rural Galilee. Many have to do with Galilee's agriculture, because almost everyone was engaged in cultivation in some form or another. "The Kingdom of God," Jesus explained, "is like a mustard seed, the smallest of all seeds on earth, that, when sown, becomes the greatest of all shrubs" (Matthew 13:31). Or "the Kingdom of God is like a seed that sprouts while the farmer is asleep; it grows into a stalk, the head, and finally the grain, which the farmer cuts with his sickle" (Mark 4:26–29). The Apostles must have nodded, but it is doubtful that they grasped what Jesus was talking about. Other parables take their cue from the debts that many farmers struggled with, or the egregious gap between rich and poor, such as the story of the Talents and Pounds (Matthew 25:14–30), the Creditor (Luke 7:41–43), the Rich Fool (Luke 12:16–21), and the Pharisee and the Tax Collector (Luke 18:9–14). Some parables explore the importance of family and clan in Galilee, such as the story of Two Sons (Matthew 21:28–31), the Prodigal Son (Luke 15:11–32), and the Wedding Banquet (Matthew 22:1–14).

Time and again, Jesus tells these rather mysterious stories. In most cases, the deeper symbolic meaning is not always obvious, and many parables leave the Apostles befuddled. In the case of the parable of the Sower, for example, the Apostles must have been particularly clueless, because Jesus said to them, somewhat exasperated, "Do you not understand this parable? Then how will you understand all the parables?" He then explained what he was trying to say. "The sower sows the *word*," he said. "These are the ones on the path where the word is sown: when they hear, Satan immediately comes and takes away the word that is sown in them." Similarly, the word may fall on rocky soil, that is, among people who only have a superficial interest. In that case, "when trouble or persecution arises on account of the word, immediately they fall away" (Mark 4:15–20).

The parables take up so much of the Gospel literature that the genre has spawned a separate movement of biblical scholarship, which continues to debate their meaning. One reason is their sheer diversity. Amazingly, only five parables are listed in all three Synoptic Gospels. Matthew has nine parables that don't appear anywhere else, while Luke includes no less than twelve parables that are unique to his Gospel. So the underlying oral traditions about Jesus' parables must have been vast.

Taken together, the Kingdom parables also set up an essential conflict: that between Jesus and the Jewish authorities, particularly the priestly group of the Sadducees, who had a very different idea about what redemption in Judaism meant. For the Sadducees, the Jerusalem Temple was the only place of salvation, and the combination of tithes and sacrificial rites was the only way to secure it. That is why some scholars believe that the parables are essentially "subversive."[7] It may also be the reason why Jesus couches his sermons about the Kingdom of God in the veiled language of simple, folksy stories: he was well aware of the risks he was taking if, indeed, his teachings were perceived as an attack on the established order. In the Gospel of Mark, Jesus even states quite plainly that he is comfortable talking about the Kingdom of God with his Apostles, but not with "those outside" his immediate circle of followers. For those outsiders, he says, "everything comes in parables in order that they may indeed look, but not perceive, and may indeed listen, but not understand" (Mark 4:11–12).

But even his Apostles struggled to follow what Jesus was saying. And then Jesus decided on another tack. Just like we

teach our children simple nursery rhymes, he taught his followers a simple Aramaic prayer of seven lines.

Abba	Our Father
Yǝtqadaš šǝmak.	hallowed be your name.
Teṭe malkuṭak.	Your kingdom come.
Pitṭan dǝ-ṣorak hav lan yomǝden.	Give us each day our daily bread.
wa-Švuq lan ḥovenan	And forgive us our debts,
Hek ʿǝnan šǝvaqin lǝ-ḥaivenan.	as we forgive our debtors.
wǝ-La taʿel lan lǝ-nisyon.[8]	And do not bring us to the test.
	(Luke 11:2–4)

There are several reasons why, in the next part of this book, I
describe the version that appears in Luke, rather than the one
featured in Matthew's Gospel (Matthew 6:5–15). Most scholars
agree that the Lucan prayer was probably closest to the Aramaic
original formulated by Jesus, and that this original found its way
into the sayings document known as Q. Matthew, like Luke,
then adopted the prayer from Q but embellished it with interpolations. These interpolations—such as, "Your will be done on
earth as it is in heaven"—could have been added to the prayer
by early Christian communities.

As Sinclair Bugeja wrote, in its structure Luke's version follows the precedent of prayers and Psalms in Hebrew Scripture.
It opens with (1) an address to God, followed by (2) two divine
imperatives regarding the holiness of God and the establishment
of the kingdom, and lastly, (3) three human petitions for (a) necessary provisions, (b) the forgiveness of sins/debts, and (c) the
release from the "test."[9] But in its formulation and meaning, the
prayer is unique in the biblical literature. Indeed, both Matthew

and Luke suggest that this was a prayer that Jesus himself used before he chose to share it with his followers.

Today, Christians all know this prayer; many of us recite it every Sunday. But do we understand what Jesus is saying? Do we really grasp the depth, meaning, and modern-day relevancy of these simple words?

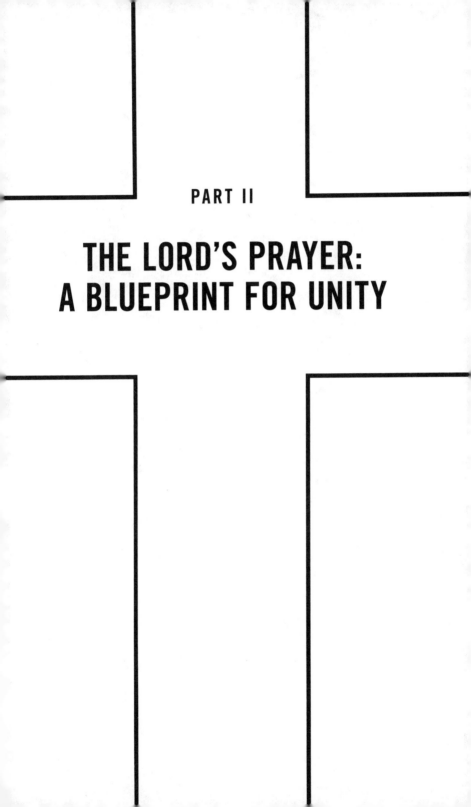

PART II

THE LORD'S PRAYER: A BLUEPRINT FOR UNITY

| 5 |

OUR FATHER, HALLOWED BE YOUR NAME

In ancient Judaism, the name of God played a unique role. Unlike the cults and religions that surrounded Israel during the Iron Age and the Classical Era, Judaism refused to allow anyone to depict God in painting or sculpture. That was rather unprecedented. In Canaan, the god *El* was worshipped in the shape of a bull. In Egypt, gods were depicted in a variety of forms, as humans, animals, or a combination of both. And the Greeks and Romans believed that the gods were similar to human beings but with a physical beauty that put them far above mere mortals. That is why sculptures of deities such as Apollo or Venus are carved with such astonishing perfection. When early Christianity moved out of Roman Palestine and into the empire at large, it inherited these expectations, because people in Asia Minor, Greece, and Rome were used to *seeing* the god they were praying to. It is for that reason that the earliest depictions of Jesus appear not in Judea or Galilee proper, but in the catacombs of Rome or on Christian sarcophagi uncovered in Turkey. Depictions of God, as well as the Apostles and the saints, soon followed.

In sum, Europeans who had been conditioned by centuries of Greek and Roman iconography needed what in German is called an *Andachtsbild*, a devotional image. In contrast, ancient Judaism in the time of Jesus did not tolerate such a tradition.

That may also be the reason that in Jewish worship, the name by which people prayed to God has a very special meaning, for it was only through this form of address that believers could turn their mind to the divine. According to Genesis, simple, spontaneous prayer *(tefillah)* originated almost from the beginning. "People began to call on the name of the Lord," says the Book of Genesis, speaking of the generations that came after Adam and Eve (Genesis 4:26). The verb "to pray" then appears in the story of Abraham. After King Abimelech takes Sarah as

| *A fourth-century sarcophagus depicting a beardless Jesus with his Apostles.*

a mistress, believing (as did Pharaoh) that she is Abraham's sister rather than his wife, God turns to the king in a dream and tells him: "Now then, return the man's wife; for he is a prophet, and he will pray for you and you will live" (Genesis 20:7). Later on, Abraham did pray to God, and "God healed Abimelech, and also healed his wife and female slaves so that they could have children again" (Genesis 20:17).

From that point on, prayer becomes the primary venue for seeking intercession from God. When Abraham sends his servant to find a wife for his son Isaac from among his kin in Harran, the servant prays that whichever girl gives him a drink at the well will be the woman who will marry Isaac (Genesis 24:15). This girl is Rebekah, and later, after her marriage to Isaac, her husband will pray to the Lord to open her womb and allow her to conceive a child (Genesis 24:51). Other women in the Bible will likewise pray for a child, such as Rachel, Hannah, and Elizabeth, and their prayers, too, will be heard.

It is interesting that, unlike our modern practice of whispering prayers, or reciting them silently in our heart, prayers were usually spoken aloud in biblical times. This was true for most ancient peoples, who tended to address their deities in a loud voice. When Hannah was found to be praying silently at the shrine of Shiloh, and "only her lips moved, but her voice was not heard," she caused quite a stir. A priest named Eli denounced her, saying, "How long will you make a drunken spectacle of yourself? Put away your wine." In reply, Hannah said, "No, my lord, I am a woman deeply troubled; I have drunk neither wine nor strong drink, but I have been pouring out my soul before the Lord" (1 Samuel 1:13–15).

In Jesus' time, villagers would gather on the Sabbath in a designated place such as the threshing floor, the village well, or perhaps a prayer room (*proseuchè* in Greek) to share in prayer, honoring the commandment in Deuteronomy to "to serve [the Lord] with all your heart and with all your soul" (Deuteronomy 11:13). It is not clear whether they would have sung hymns as well, as in modern Jewish worship, but Jesus was certainly familiar with the Psalms, which are essentially prayers to be sung or set to music. Some of the early sources from the Book of Psalms even include what we think are musical notations.

But how did the Jews in Jesus' time address God? In the Torah, the first division of Hebrew Scripture, God is referred to by two names: the four-letter construct known as YHWH (Yahweh) or the title *El* and its plural, *Elohim*. Some two centuries before Jesus, the term *Adonai* became the accepted form, which in English is usually translated as "the Lord," a custom that would be continued in the Gospels. Finally, in the first century, another form of address emerged: *Ha-Shem,* literally "the Name"—a term as mysterious as God itself.

Which name would Jesus have used? After all, Joseph and Mary spoke Aramaic. The answer is probably the Aramaic version of *Elohim*, which is *Elahiy* or *Elahah*. The Gospel of Mark says that in his final moments on the cross, Jesus exclaimed, in Aramaic, the opening verse from Psalm 22: *Eloi, Eloi, lema sabachthani?*—"My God, my God, why have you forsaken me?" (Mark 15:34; Psalms 22:1). Of course, Mark wrote in Greek. Consequently, *Eloi* is most likely a Greek transliteration of the Aramaic *Elahiy.*

Another way to answer this question is to consider what modern scholarship has called the "Jewishness" of Jesus. In our modern times, we so often see Jesus in isolation, as the Son of God who came down from heaven to be crucified, and through this sacrifice on the cross, redeem all of humankind. But historically,

Jesus was much more than that. Even though his teachings would become the foundation of a new religion, Christianity, historians today recognize that Jesus' ministry unfolded in a fundamentally Jewish context. We only have to read the Gospels to know that Jesus observed the Torah and often taught from the Books of the Prophets, the Hebrew Bible division known as the *Nevi'im*. So did his parents: Mary observed the period of uncleanliness following the birth of her son as specified in Leviticus, and then traveled to Jerusalem to offer a sacrifice as a burnt offering "and a pigeon or a turtledove for a sin offering" (Leviticus 12:2–7). When Jesus was twelve years old, he and his parents joined a group of villagers on a journey to Jerusalem to observe the Passover festival, "according to the custom" (Luke 2:41–2). And when Jesus began his ministry, he was recognized as a rabbi, a teacher of the Torah (John 1:38).

But Jesus approached the Torah in a very personal and individual way. Like the Prophets Amos and Hosea before him, he emphasized the need for faith, rather than the idea that one could expiate one's sins through animal sacrifice—"I desire mercy and not sacrifice, and the knowledge of God rather than burnt offerings" (Hosea 6:6). Jesus quotes those very words in the Gospel of Matthew, and nowhere do we see Jesus performing any sacrificial rite (Matthew 9:13).

That is why Jesus came up with an entirely novel and rather radical way to refer to God. He did not call him *Adonai* or *Ha-Shem* but, quite simply, "Papa," or *Abba* (the word is similar in Hebrew as in Aramaic). That doesn't mean, however, that God's name should be any less revered or treated with respect, because in the same breadth the Lucan version of the prayer says *Abba Yǝtqadaš šǝmak,* "Our Papa, Hallowed be Your Name." Here, Jesus harks back to the *Shema,* the Jewish profession of faith: "Hear, O Israel! Adonai is our God! Adonai is One! Blessed be the name of His glorious kingdom for ever and ever."

By calling God *Abba,* Jesus tried to eliminate the great distance that existed between God and the Jews of his time. It is true that the term "Father" also appears in Hebrew Scripture with regards to God, but in a sense that God is the father of the twelve tribes of Israel (Exodus 4:22; Isaiah 63:16; and Hosea 11:1, for example). Jesus' use of *Abba,* however, implies a deep bond with God, analogous to the use of "Dad" or "Daddy" in English, and that was unprecedented. With his prayer, Jesus sought to forge a deep intimacy between God and the individual, which would have been a shock for many Jews of his time.

For Jesus, YHWH is not some austere deity to be placated with animal flesh, but a loving father to whom he could confide his innermost fears and dreams—and he wanted his followers, including us, to feel the same way. This feeling of intimacy with the Divine, this sense of God as a personal mentor, may have been nurtured by Jesus' sense of estrangement from his family and village. Scholars, including Bruce Chilton, have suggested that Jesus grew up under a cloud in his village because of his uncertain paternity—at least in the eyes of the villagers. As Luke and Matthew tell us, Mary was pregnant with Jesus before she was wed to Joseph. According to Deuteronomy, such a child was designated a *mamzer,* doomed to be ostracized from the congregation and social life. The Mishnah, too, castigates *mamzers* as children born of an illegitimate sexual union.[1] Christians, of course, know that Mary was conceived by the Holy Spirit, but that would not have been obvious to the people in a small, gossip-ridden hamlet like Nazareth. Chilton believes that it would have had a profound psychological impact on the development of the young Jesus. The other children in the village would have been discouraged from playing with him. If Jesus was allowed to attend prayer gatherings at all, he would have been prevented from speaking up. It is not difficult to imagine that under these circumstances, Jesus developed a very strong and intimate bond with God, which would have blossomed in the months and years of his solitary wandering from village to village as a young rabbi. We get that sense of estrangement from his immediate family when Jesus says in Luke, "Whoever comes to me and does not hate father and mother, wife and children, brothers and sisters, yes, and even life itself, cannot be my disciple" (Luke 14:26–27).

In a very real sense, then, God was Jesus' father and confidant, both on earth and in heaven. He was a Dad on whose shoulders Jesus could rest his weary head, no matter where he found himself. Here again, I believe that Jesus may have found inspiration in the words of Jeremiah. If indeed he was educated as a rabbi, he would have been deeply familiar with both the Torah and the Books of the Prophets. Jeremiah was a man who found himself in a period very similar to Jesus', a time of a deep social chasm between the poor and the elites, and as a result Jeremiah experienced the same close bond with God. Jeremiah, too, advocated a simpler, purer form of Judaism that went back to the very roots of Israel's raison d'être: to be a community of equals under the eyes of a compassionate God. Jeremiah wanted to return Judaism to its core spirituality, albeit a "naked spirituality," in the words of one of Jeremiah's biographers, devoid of the pitfalls of wealth, power, and inequality.[2]

| 6 |

YOUR KINGDOM COME

Perhaps the most stirring, yet also the most enigmatic verse in the *Our Father* is the phrase "Your Kingdom Come." As Christians we recite this verse every Sunday—but do we really know what it means? Have we ever paused to think what "Kingdom" Jesus is talking about? Is this realm on earth, or in heaven?

I have been a practicing Christian all my life, but I can't remember when Jesus' Kingdom was the sole topic of a Sunday sermon. And that's rather sad when you think that Jesus' Kingdom vision is front and center in his teachings. The Gospels are full of references to the Kingdom, and the same philosophy returns, time and again, in Jesus' parables. So why don't we try to understand what Jesus is telling us?

I think the answer is twofold. One, our idea who Jesus was, and what his ministry was about, is largely shaped by Paul—or Saul (*Sha'ul*) as he was originally called—since his letters are the earliest Christian documents extant today. Paul was not born in

Galilee but in the city of Tarsus, the capital of Cilicia (today's southern Turkey). As a result, his worldview was not informed by the unique conditions in first-century Galilee, but by the Greco-Roman culture that permeated the city. "The inhabitants of Tarsus have become so enthusiastic for philosophy and the area of education," wrote the first-century Roman geographer Strabo, "that they have surpassed Athens, Alexandria, and any other place."[1]

The son of a family that made a living as tent makers or leather workers, Saul claimed to have been educated as a Pharisee (Philippians 3:5). According to the Book of Acts of the Apostles, he was even taught in Jerusalem by the distinguished rabbi Gamaliel, a leading Pharisaic sage, and possibly the same Gamaliel who had intervened on Peter's behalf during his interrogation by the Sanhedrin. In other words, Saul was everything that the Apostles were not: an intellectual. Worldly, fluent in Greek, and steeped in Hebrew Scripture as well as Greek philosophy and ethics, Saul tried to make a name for himself among the Temple authorities by vigorously persecuting Jesus' followers after the crucifixion. But he changed his mind during a campaign to root out Christian followers in Damascus (Acts 9:4) and became a convert to the Jesus movement.

To say that the Apostles viewed that conversion with suspicion is perhaps an understatement. Most followers believed he was a fifth columnist, trying to infiltrate the movement so as to eviscerate it from within. The Greek faction, which had temporarily gained the upper hand in the Apostolic movement, even tried to assassinate him (Acts 9:26–29). In response, Saul withdrew from the Jerusalem group and decided to go his own way. And that is a tragic outcome, because Saul had never met Jesus in the flesh. He had never heard his stirring oratory, nor experienced the sheer power of his presence. And because Saul was largely shunned by the Apostles, he was rarely given the opportunity to hear, first-hand, from witnesses who *did* know Jesus intimately and could have given him detailed accounts of his ministry. "I did not confer with any human being, nor did I go up to Jerusalem to those who were already Apostles before me," he wrote in his letter to the Galatians (1:17). And so Saul decided to develop his own idea as to who Jesus was and what his ministry meant for humankind.

That concept didn't happen overnight, of course. It was gradually shaped by the reception that Saul received as he tried to do what the Apostles were doing in Judea, namely, to preach—in his case, to the Greco-Roman world of Asia Minor. To begin with, he changed his name from the Jewish *Sha'ul* to the Latinized *Paulus*, demonstrating his willingness to adapt his message to a Greco-Roman audience. But as he began his journeys, Paul was in for a shock. Almost all Jewish communities he encountered firmly rejected the idea that Jesus could be the Jewish *Mashiach*, the Messiah (translated as *Christos* in Greek, or "Christ" in English). How could a man who had been tried and executed as a rebel by the Roman authorities be recognized as the Messiah? Unlike many Jews in Roman Palestine, the Jewish communities of the Diaspora didn't feel oppressed by the Romans and were quite content to live under the *Pax Romana*. For the first time in centuries, there was peace in the Mediterranean world. The pirates who had preyed on seaborne trade for so long had been vanquished. All of the world traded in the same coin, the *denarius*. And all were ruled by Roman law.

What's more, had not Caesar and Augustus specifically excused the Jews from worship to Rome's pagan gods? Were Jews not exempt from military service? And did not the sophisticated apparatus of the Roman Empire facilitate the collection of tithes for the *korban*, the treasury of the Temple in Jerusalem? Why, then, should Jews jeopardize the special privileges they enjoyed by embracing a man marked as a terrorist by Rome? Besides, Judaism already had its savior, its law-giver, and his name was Moses.

Wherever Paul went, accompanied by assistants such as Barnabas, Silas, or Timothy, his preaching was angrily rebuffed. The Jewish community of Lystra even tried to stone him. But at the same time, another pattern was emerging. Whereas most Jews refused to accept his teachings, many Gentiles were quite receptive.

What attracted these Gentiles? Simply put, it was the exquisite nobility of a religion that recognized but one God. A truly merciful and compassionate God, moreover, who cared for his people, unlike the capricious gods of Roman mythology. While the empire may have enjoyed peace, there were still thousands of men and women, both freedman and slave, who yearned for an end to the senseless social divisions of the Roman world. And so, it is not difficult to imagine that these people would have felt a deep attraction to the portrait of a man who said that the righteous would ultimately find salvation—and performed miracles to prove it. And given the absurd imperial cult that worshiped each emperor as a god upon his death and compelled people to offer sacrifices to them, it seems that the Roman world was ripe for a new spirituality, a *genuine* spirituality.

In response, Paul began to shift the nature of Jesus as the Jewish Messiah—a term that would have made no sense to Gentiles—to that of the universal Son of God. Romans understood the concept of "Son of God." Their world was filled with depictions of gods and demigods, including their mortal offspring. But Paul was careful to define the relationship of Jesus to God in Jewish terms. In contrast to Luke's later Nativity narrative, Paul's letter to the Romans argues that Jesus' biological lineage ran from Joseph all the way back to David "according to the flesh" (Romans 1:3). It was only by virtue of his resurrection from the dead, by the power of the Spirit, that he became the Son of God. This idea—which historians refer to as the Pauline *kerygma*—became an article of faith in the nascent Christian communities that Paul and his followers were trying to build. In fact, it is a bedrock of faith for most Christian traditions today.

The problem with the Pauline kerygma is that it largely ignores the Jewish and Galilean context of Jesus' ministry, as well as the very principles that Jesus was trying to articulate. This was a deliberate choice, because Paul quickly realized that the Jewish framework of Jesus' ministry was a major deterrent for many Gentiles. Back in Judea, Apostles like Peter were quite happy to convert Gentiles provided they *also* become observant Jews. This became the crux of growing tensions between Paul's activity in Asia Minor and the Apostolic movement in Judea. If a Gentile was to be baptized, was he also expected to behave as a Jew? Should he abide by the Jewish Law? Should his food be kosher—an important question, particularly since the early Eucharist was becoming a key feature of Early Christianity? And lastly, was he expected to be circumcised as well?

The original Apostles, who remained practicing Jews, felt the answer was *yes*. For them, faith in Jesus was inseparable from Jesus' own example as a Jewish rabbi. But Paul felt otherwise. He believed that the Jewish rite of circumcision had now been replaced by baptism and faith in Christ. "Real circumcision is a matter of the heart," he wrote; "it is spiritual, not literal" (Romans 2:29). Or to put it differently, "a person is justified not by the works of the Law but through faith in Jesus Christ" (Galatians 2:16). Therefore, Gentiles who agreed to be baptized did *not* need to be circumcised or follow the kosher laws and rules of ritual purity. They could remain Roman Gentiles, rather than Jews.

It follows, then, that whatever Jesus had said or preached as part of his ministry in Jewish Galilee, at a time of a great socio-economic crisis, was less relevant to Paul's evangelizing campaign in the Roman Empire than his Christology. In effect, Paul unmoored the Jesus movement from its Jewish roots altogether, and made it a new religion uniquely suited to the needs and aspirations of the Roman world. What had begun as a reform movement by a rabbi in Jewish Galilee was now separating itself from that tradition. But we should be thankful that Paul—and many other missionaries like him—acted the way he did. Without their evangelizing, we may have never heard about Jesus. The original movement in Judea, now led by Jesus' brother James, was bound to succumb to the fierce persecution by the Temple authorities. Indeed, by the time the First Jewish Revolt broke out in 66 CE, Jewish Christians in Galilee and Judea had increasingly become ostracized from their synagogues and communities.

But we should not ignore what Jesus himself had to say on the question of why he began his ministry. In fact, from the very beginning Jesus made the purpose of his activism very clear. As we saw, upon launching his ministry in the synagogue of Nazareth, Jesus recited from Isaiah, saying, "The Spirit of the Lord is upon me, for he has anointed me; he has sent me to bring good news to the oppressed, and heal the brokenhearted" (Isaiah 61:1–2). And then Jesus added, "Today this scripture has been fulfilled in your hearing" (Luke 4:21). The Gospel of Mark, the oldest Gospel, phrases this "mission statement" even more succinctly: "The time is fulfilled, and the kingdom of God has come near; repent, and believe in the good news" (Mark 1:15).

And this brings us to the second reason why we hear so little about Jesus' Kingdom of God in today's worship. Many Jewish prophets had talked about a "reign of God" in the preceding centuries (for example, Chronicles 16:33; Isaiah 26:21; and Micah 1:3). They saw it as a nation governed by Jewish Law and ruled by a true and legitimate Davidic king, rather than a Herodian tyrant or a Roman despot. What's more, Jesus' movement was not the only one that went around preaching renewal. There were many others, such as followers of John the Baptist, or the Essenes, or the community of Qumran—or the much-reviled Pharisees, at least in the eyes of the evangelists. The Jewish historian Josephus even lists several preachers who, like Jesus, were also miracle workers who preached the coming of God's Kingdom, such as a character named "Honi the Circle Drawer" and a man named Hanina ben Dosa.

All of these factions offered their followers a promise: the prospect of redemption in the form of a new society, a new *kingdom* based on the principles of the Torah, the Jewish Law. So what made Jesus' Kingdom of God so unique? And why did his teachings find such an extraordinary response among the people of Galilee? For me, these are the urgent questions that lie at the heart of the tension—real or imagined—between the Jesus of history and the Christ of faith. And only by answering these questions can we begin to truly understand what made the ministry of Jesus so exceptional—and so revolutionary.

To do so, we must first recognize the unique social and cultural context of his time. All of the institutions that support our lives today were unheard of in Jesus' time. Housing, water wells, threshing floors, food supply, worship, and mutual protection were all the responsibility of the family and the village community in which one lived. Schools—at least in rural

Galilee—were few. Local roads were built by the village that relied on them to bring its produce to market. None of these services was forthcoming from the state, even though most states in Antiquity, including Roman Palestine, taxed their populations mercilessly. This also explains why being ostracized from one's village because of a chronic illness, a frequent occurrence in the Gospels, was tantamount to a death sentence.

Furthermore, the world of ancient Palestine was a class society, with a clear and distinct hierarchy of social ranks. At the top stood the ruler, who in the time of Jesus was really a vassal lord like Antipas who served at the pleasure of Rome. Below the ruler came a thin layer of aristocracy, which in Jesus' lifetime included both noblemen associated with the old Hasmonean dynasty, as well as the "new men" who owed their wealth and status to the patronage of Herod and his sons, or to their collaboration with Roman governors. The caste of chief priests attached to the Temple formed another aristocratic elite. This included the high priest, who in the time of Jesus was appointed by the Romans and therefore believed by many Jews—rightly or wrongly—to be doing the Roman prefect's bidding.

Under the nobility came another thin layer of the professional class, men who were literate, educated, and trained to hold any number of positions in local government. Many of these laymen were Pharisees. Others were in private practice as a notary or scribe, to whom one turned for marriage contracts or the transfer of land deeds. Since the prevailing law in Palestine was a religious law, the Torah, these scribes were of necessity also schooled in religious matters. This is why the Gospels often depict Jesus in debate with both Pharisees and scribes on any number of religious topics.

Beneath the small professional class came the vast majority of illiterate peasants and day workers, who made up the bulk of Galilee's population—by some estimates, as much as 90 percent. This also included the great mass of the poor, the unemployed, and the disabled—including those stricken by disease or injured veterans from wars and rebellions, such as the revolts that ravaged Galilee in the first decade of Jesus' life.

And this is the crux of the matter. As we saw in previous chapters, Jesus' ministry unfolded in a crisis very similar to the one we are battling today. This explains why Jesus' parables are filled with characters that rarely appear in previous Jewish writings, such as the *phronimoi* or *oikonomoi,* usually translated in English as "stewards" or "managers," who are running large estates on behalf of rich landowners in Jerusalem. Many local peasants had no choice but to accept work as *georgoi,* as tenant farmers, on the same land that had once belonged to them. In one of Jesus' parables, he spoke of a rich man who "produced abundantly. And he thought to himself, 'What should I do, for I have no place to store my crops?' Then he said, 'I will do this: I will pull down my barns and build larger ones, and there I will store all my grain and my goods. And I will say to my soul, "Soul, you have ample goods laid up for many years; relax, eat, drink, be merry."' But God said to him, 'You fool! This very night your life is being demanded of you. And the things you have prepared, whose will they be?'" (Luke 12:16–20). In another telling parable, a group of tenant farmers are so fed up with their lot that they beat the servants of the landowner sent to collect the harvest (Mark 12:2–5). Much of this tax policy was continued by Herod's son Antipas in order to fund the construction of the cities of Sepphoris and Tiberias in Galilee.

| *The Beit Netofa Valley in Galilee.*

In response, the Sermon on the Mount depicts a Jesus who is determined to fundamentally change the way people behave toward one other, by virtue of one simple expedient: *agápē* or "love." "Love your enemies," he says in Matthew's Gospel, but for a specific purpose: to "do good to those who hate you, bless those who curse you, pray for those who abuse you" (Matthew 5:44–45). In other words, try to combat evil with love. After all, Jesus argues, "if you love those who love you, what credit is that to you? For even sinners love those who love them" (Luke 6:27–28). These are the words of a Jesus we recognize—words that anchor the quintessential tenets of the Kingdom of God.

And this also shows what makes Jesus' Kingdom so different from that envisioned by his precursors. Whereas most of Jesus' contemporaries (including John the Baptist) believed that the reign of God would only come about as a result of some great cataclysm or violent regime change, Jesus saw it quite differently. At its core was a new social covenant whereby Jews pledged to live with compassion and solidarity within one's community and profess an overarching love and faith in God.

Jesus' Kingdom of God, in sum, was a program of social and spiritual revolution, a grassroots movement of people power, rather than a plan for political change. Indeed, many Gospel passages suggest that Jesus believed the kingdom would evolve spontaneously in his lifetime, regardless of the secular authority that happened to rule the nation (Mark 1:15; Luke 17:21).

Was Jesus, a Jewish rabbi, moving beyond the boundaries of the Torah in propagating his Kingdom of God? Jesus would have argued that he did not. "Do not think," he says in the closing coda of Matthew's Sermon, "that I have come to abolish the law and the prophets," referring to the two divisions that formed the canon of Hebrew Scripture in his time; "I have come not to abolish but to fulfill" (Matthew 5:17). In other words, Jesus did not see his vision of the Kingdom as a break with contemporary Judaism. On the contrary, for him the Kingdom was a restoration of Judaism's most cherished values—social responsibility, moral living, and faithfulness to God.

Unfortunately, in modern Christian liturgy, Jesus' revolutionary concept of the Kingdom is often misunderstood or ignored. Part of the reason is that later Christian authors read the Kingdom teachings outside of their social and historical context—indeed, devoid of their Jewish framework altogether. As a result, Christian traditions began to see the Kingdom as a prophesy of the heavenly paradise that awaits faithful followers after death. This notion is partly abetted by the fact that Jesus' statements about the Kingdom, including his parables, are often ambiguous, with subtle differences among the Gospels themselves. Even today, particularly in public discourse, many politicians who declare themselves as Christians tend to ignore Jesus' core message of social compassion, particularly toward those who are "poor and brokenhearted." And yet, the yawning gap between rich and poor in our modern times is not unlike that which Jesus witnessed in his own day.

In sum, there is little question that for Jesus, the Kingdom doctrine was the guiding purpose of his mission: to bring about a revolution of the heart, with real and tangible implications for the people of his time. It charged his followers with a personal commitment to bridge the deep social and economic chasm of his time. And that message is particularly urgent in our day, particularly in the United States where the top 1 percent holds over $25 trillion in wealth, more than that owned by the bottom 80 percent.

If we want to call ourselves Christians, we have to be prepared to do what Jesus asks us to do. Being a Christian is not just about ourselves; it's not just about securing our own salvation in anticipation of our reward in heaven. Jesus calls us to go out and be a force of moral good, in our families, our workplace, and the communities in which we live. More than any other Jewish preacher of his time, Jesus was deeply concerned with the social injustices of Lower Galilee, particularly the rampant hunger, poverty, and displacement among the Galilean peasantry (Luke 6:20–23). This urged new priorities, and the need for the spirit, rather than the letter, of the Torah to be followed. Or as he puts it in the Gospel of Mark, "The Sabbath was made for humankind, not humankind for the Sabbath" (Mark 2:27). Many years later, the Talmud would make the same point.

But Jesus never translated this mission into political or revolutionary activism, notwithstanding the effort by some scholars to see him as such. Unlike other protest movements of his era, Jesus tried to avoid any conflict with the Romans. According to Luke, he was once asked, "Is it lawful for us to pay taxes to the emperor, or not?" This was a highly sensitive issue, because the tax census of 6 CE—when Jesus would have been about ten years old—had elicited a revolt. In response, Jesus asked for a coin, a *denarius*, and replied, "Give to the emperor the things that are the emperor's, and to God the thing that are God's" (Luke 20:22–24).

For Jesus, the political sphere and the socio-religious sphere were separate; one never needed to come into conflict with the other. This is the reason why, time and again, Jesus reaches out to the elites of the land, and why he winds up dining with tax collectors and other powerful individuals. They were the ones responsible for the extreme social divides in Galilee. Consequently, they were in a position to correct it.

"I have not come to call the righteous," he said, "but the sick" (Mark 2:17).

One would think that Jesus' call for building a more equitable and compassionate society would have tremendous relevance in a world that is devastated by the COVID pandemic, climate change, and the increasing competition for scarce resources. But surprisingly, that is not the case. Many of our Christian communities remain focused on our culture wars and the attempt to legislate what should or should not happen in our bedrooms, and indeed the most intimate aspects of our lives. Yet, when other cultures try to impose such rules—such as the tenets of Shari'ah Law in nations like Iran—we call it an egregious denial of human rights and individual freedom.

The real question is, what would Jesus expect us to do when 10.7 percent of our nation (or the equivalent of thirty-eight million Americans) live below the poverty line?[2] Would he have endorsed a platform that calls for restrictions on Medicaid, on food stamps or other programs for the poor?[3]

And what would Jesus say about the fact that twenty-seven million non-elderly Americans have no health insurance, even though our nation is still trying to recover from the greatest health crisis in a century?[4] As a man who devoted so much of his ministry to healing the sick, would Jesus have approved of attempts to deny Americans the most basic of human rights: the right to health and wellness?

Jesus' passionate advocacy for the Kingdom of God should remind us that being a Christian—that is, to walk in the footsteps of Jesus—is not about being liberal or conservative. It is about creating a more compassionate society for all of God's children, regardless of their race, culture, sexual orientation, or social condition.

| 7 |

GIVE US EACH DAY OUR BREAD

Bread figures prominently in the Bible. The Hebrew *Hamotzi*, the "Blessing over Bread" recited during the Shabbat dinner, says: "Blessed are you, Lord, God of all creation. Through your goodness we have this bread to offer, which earth has given and human hands have made. It will become for us the bread of life." Jesus quotes from this prayer when he breaks bread with his Apostles during the Last Supper.

Just as in the Western world, bread is a staple of every person's diet in the Middle East. Then and now, most bread consumed in the Middle East is leavened flatbread, or pita bread. Bread can be made in any manner of ways, but in Jesus' time it was made by pouring several cups of grain into a mill, which consisted of two round slabs of stone, anchored on a central wooden spike. This allowed the woman of the household to move the top slab back and forth across the bottom slab by way of a wooden handle. The motion crushed kernels and ground them into a fine flour that then sifted down to the floor. For a young mother like Mary, it was hard work: one hour of grinding would typically produce only some 800 grams of flour. She then collected the flour in a bowl and added a bit of salt, a few drops of olive oil, and half a cup of water, kneading the mixture until it had the consistency of dough. She also added yeast—the spoiled remains of dough from two days back—to leaven the bread so it would rise in the oven. When Jesus was young, he must have observed his mother preparing the dough because during his later ministry he would compare the Kingdom of Heaven to "yeast that a woman took and mixed in with three measures of flour, until all of it was leavened" (Matthew 13:33).

Once the dough was ready, Mary's agile hands quickly shaped it into thin round cakes, which baked more quickly and thus saved time and fuel. Then it was time to fire the oven. Like most women, Mary probably used animal dung to fire her oven, with branches and leaves for kindling. Once it was lit, she waited until the small clay chamber above the fire was sufficiently hot. She then placed the cakes on a wooden palette and slid the cakes into the baking chamber, checking regularly to ensure that the bread rose and baked to her liking. A reconstruction of an ancient "kitchen" in a typical Galilean house, built in Qatzrin in Upper Galilee, illustrates this process. Thus, as the sun rose, a Galilean family would gather in the courtyard and enjoy their first meal of the day—delicious hot bread, dipped in olive oil and seasoned with a bit of garlic—while sitting on rough woolen rugs, as many families in the Middle East still do today.

That same bread then served as a quick snack at midday and at suppertime, the second and last meal of the day, when the bread would be augmented with a cooked egg or vegetable.

Interior of a kitchen with a flour mill and an oven from the reconstructed village in Qatzrin.

Only on the Sabbath would the family eat three meals. Later rabbinic writings specified that a Sabbath meal should include at least two cooked foods to underscore the festive character of this holy day—for example, fried fish, legume paste, or vegetables.[1]

Grains were, of course, in great demand, for bread was the main staple of the Galilean diet. That is why Joseph and other farmers planted wheat and barley in late November. Wheat was used for bread, whereas barley was served as fodder for farm animals. In times of drought or hardship, barley would be used for bread as well, though it contained far less vitamins, as we saw. Sometime in February, during the Jewish month of Adar, young Jesus would have seen the first sprouts of barley appear. By April (*Nisan/Iyyar*) these ears would be ready for harvesting. The wheat harvest followed a month later. The reaping was done with a scythe, and all the sheaves were stacked in the fields, or near Joseph's house, to await their turn at the threshing floor.

Every agricultural village had such a floor, which was usually a flat surface in a high position, to catch the winds. First Joseph passed over the sheaves with a device known as a threshing board, essentially a wooden slab studded with jagged stones or iron bits on the bottom. The repeated motion of the threshing board steadily removed the kernels of grain from the stalks, leaving a pile of grain, chaff (husks and stubble), and straw, all mixed together. Joseph then threw the harvested wheat up in the air, in the hope that the wind would blow away the empty stalks and chaff from the heavier kernels. In his sermons, John the Baptist used the analogy of the threshing process to describe the coming of a Messiah: his "winnowing fork is in his hand, to clear his threshing floor and to gather the wheat into his granary; but the chaff he will burn with unquenchable fire" (Luke 3:17).

| *Reconstruction of an ancient threshing board.*

As an observant Jew Joseph left the stalks at the corners of his field intact, so that they could be gleaned by the poor, observing the injunction by Leviticus to "leave [the corners] for the poor and for the foreigner residing among you" (Leviticus 23:22). Then, to mark the end of the grain harvest, farmers would celebrate the Festival of Weeks (*Shavuot,* also known as the Feast of Reaping, the Festival of First Fruits, or Pentecost).

Not surprisingly, bread also features prominently in the Gospels, with over 60 references. When Jesus sends out his Apostles, "two by two," he orders them to "take nothing for their journey except a staff; no bread, no bag, no money in their belts" (Mark 6:8). In Matthew, Jesus is tempted by the devil in the desert, who challenges him to "command these stones to become loaves of bread." Jesus replies, "One does not live by bread alone, but by every word that comes from the mouth of God" (Matthew 4:3–4). In this Gospel's account of the Sermon on the Mount, Jesus asks his listeners, "Is there anyone among you who, if your child asks for bread, will give a stone?" (Matthew 7:9).

And of all his nature miracles, perhaps the most famous one is the miraculous multiplication of loaves and fishes. This miracle, also known as the "Feeding of the Five Thousand," is the only miracle described in all four Gospels (Matthew 14:13–21; Mark 6:31–44; Luke 9:10–17; and John 6:5–15). The episode is set in a large field near the shore, today believed to be the shore of Tabgha. It is dusk; the sun has begun to set on a long day in which Jesus has taught and healed large numbers of people, and now everyone is looking for something to eat. The Apostles think the solution is to simply "send the crowds away," but Jesus refuses to do so. He knows these people; they are famished and malnourished because they have no money to buy food. So he charges his Apostles to go and find something to feed them with. A search is made, but they only come up with five barley loaves and two fishes. And "taking the five loaves and the two fish, he looked up to heaven, and blessed and broke the loaves, and gave them to his disciples." And, says Mark, "all ate and were filled." And when everyone was finished, "they took up twelve baskets full of broken pieces and of fish" (Mark 6:37–43).

The significance of the story, however, is that the bread they ate was no longer made from emmer wheat but from barley (John 6:9). Barley bread lacks the vitamins A, C, and D found in wheat bread, which is why it was primarily cultivated to feed livestock. In other words, the point of the story is that people were reduced to eating animal fodder. What's more, since many peasants were deprived of their village mills and ovens, the cereal would have been poorly sieved and improperly leavened, impairing the absorption of vital minerals. That is why the verse *Pittan də-sorak hav lan yoməden*, "Give us each day our bread," is a plea for *real* bread made from wheat, not only as an essential condition of human health but also of human dignity.

Jesus often sat down with his followers as well as his antagonists to observe the ritual of breaking bread. He believed that the simple act of sharing bread created a sense of companionship and made it easier to touch on sensitive topics, such as improving the fate of the Galilean peasantry. Of course, the most important meal that he shared with his Apostles was the *Seder,* the Last Supper before his Passion. This took place shortly after sunset at the beginning of Passover, one of the holiest feasts in the liturgical year. Mark tells us that Jesus dispatched two followers to look for a place where they could have the meal, which, as we will see, suggests that the stay in

Jerusalem had not been planned in advance. The Passover meal itself required elaborate preparations, and under normal circumstances we would expect Jesus and his followers to be back in Bethany. There, no doubt, his relatives Mary and Martha had been cooking and preparing the meal since dawn, in anticipation of hosting their guests for the Seder.

The two disciples followed Jesus' instructions to the letter. They spotted a servant carrying a large jar of water, followed him back to his master's house, and boldly approached the owner, saying, "The Rabbi asks, where is a guest room where I may eat the Passover with my disciples?" (Mark 14:14). The Gospel does not tell us if this master was annoyed at having such a large group of uninvited guests at such short notice, though his wife may have been.

Preparing the Seder or Passover meal was (and still is) an elaborate process. First, the lamb meat brought back from the sacrifice at the Temple was unwrapped and roasted on skewers made of pomegranate wood, using an oven set up especially for Passover in the courtyard of the house. While on the grill, the lamb was spiced with garlic cloves and repeatedly basted with honeyed olive oil. Meanwhile, the women were busy baking cakes of unleavened bread. At the same time, they would have been preparing the bitter herbs prescribed for the Seder, such as parsley, mallows, chicory, and radishes. The purpose of these bitter herbs was to remind the Jews of their bitter time in Egypt. During the meal, the herbs would be dipped in a kind of sop called *charoseth,* consisting of various fruits pounded into a paste and mixed with vinegar and salt water. All of these items were carefully arranged in different vessels, each cleaned for this use.[2]

The actual portion of lamb meat eaten by each person during the Seder was rather small. Therefore, the women would also be busy cooking a rich stew of lentils and barley to help round out the meal. They first heated the onions, garlic, carrots, and celery in olive oil until the vegetables were soft. They then added barley and lentils, covered the pot, and allowed it to simmer.

At long last, the table was set. Deep wooden or terracotta plates with high rims were placed on the table. So were clay drinking cups, for wine was an important component of the paschal supper. The Mishnah says that in order to share Israel's joy of release on Passover night, the poorest, too, should have "no fewer than four cups of wine, and even if [the funds] come from public charity."[3] The wine consumed by Jesus and his followers would have been the usual local red variety. This wine would be mixed, one part wine to two parts water.

When the meal was ready, Jesus and his disciples reclined at the table, the followers jostling to get at Jesus' left. Jesus,

| *Terracotta plates dated to the first century recovered from Galilee.*

however, was pensive. He told them that if for any reason he could no longer be with them, they should continue this ritual of breaking bread, so as to honor his name and remember his teachings. "I confer on you, just as my Father has conferred on me, a kingdom, so that you may eat and drink at my table in my kingdom," says Jesus in Luke (Luke 22:29–30). Thus, the Last Supper became the first Eucharist (from the Greek word *eucharistia,* meaning "thanksgiving"), a rite celebrated by many Christian denominations as an integral element of their worship.

In the centuries to come, the *Last Supper* would become a dominant motif in Christian art, particularly in the refectories of monasteries such as Leonardo da Vinci's fresco in the Convent of Santa Maria delle Grazie in Milan. In virtually all of these depictions—including the scene in Mel Gibson's film *The Passion of the Christ*—Jesus is shown with a loaf of bread. None of these artists (nor Gibson, it seems) realized that this was the first day of the Week of Unleavened Bread. On this evening, the head of every Jewish household was expected to search his home and gather any remaining crumbs of *chametz*—leavened bread made from wheat, oats, or barley dough that had risen through contact with water. Not a single morsel of leaven should remain to despoil the house during the Passover feast.[4] During the next seven days, Jews all over Palestine and the Diaspora would consume the hard, cracker-like bread known as *matzo* made from unleavened dough, and remember the day when their forefathers hastily prepared to flee from Egypt with no time to wait for the dough to rise.

"I am the bread of life," Jesus says in John, underscoring the role of bread as an essential condition of human life, both in Jesus' time and in ours. That is why it is so shocking to learn that in the richest country on earth, the United States, some nine million children are still food insecure.[5]

If we want to create a Kingdom of God in our country, we must do better. We must do what Jesus asked us to do: to prioritize the health and wellbeing of the poorest and marginalized in our nation at the top of our agenda. Of course, poverty reduction isn't sexy. It doesn't work as a political slogan, and barely registers on the list of things that people vote for. As a result, politicians are encouraged to dismiss the war on poverty as something not worthy of their attention. But if we want to identify ourselves as Christians, then we should listen to what Jesus tells us. We should make the alleviation of poverty and hunger our highest priority, and remove this stain from our nation.

| 8 |

AND FORGIVE US OUR DEBTS/SINS

This last and somewhat enigmatic verse in Luke's prayer had led to all sorts of interpretations. Once again, the problem is that the original Aramaic verse, *wa-Švuq lan ḥovenan,* can mean several things. The Aramaic word *ḥova* means both "debt" and "sin." Matthew and Luke struggled with this as well. Matthew's Gospel translates *ḥovenan* (the plural form of *ḥova*) with the Greek word ὀφειλήματα (*opheilémata*), which means "debts" (Matthew 6:12). According to this view, forgiveness is seen as dispensation from debt. In Luke, however, *ḥovenan* is translated as αμαρτίας (*amartías*) or "sins," in the sense of offenses against God (Luke 11:4). We may be able to forgive their ambivalence, because the Aramaic *Targum* of the Hebrew Bible struggled with the same thing.

Before we explore this further, let's take a step back and see what language Jesus would have used to *read* the Hebrew

Bible. For centuries, the dominant language of ancient Israel was Hebrew, but that changed with the upheaval caused by the Assyrian and then Neo-Babylonian invasions. From the eighth century BCE onward, the language spoken in Assyria was Aramaic, the language of the Aramaeans that originated in Mesopotamia and shares many roots with Semitic languages, including Hebrew. In the sixth century, the Persian conquerors of Babylonia chose Aramaic as the new *lingua franca* of their realm. As a result, when Israel became a Persian possession Aramaic began to replace Hebrew as the language of the nation.

That meant that by the first century CE, hardly anyone spoke Hebrew anymore except for the scribes and scholars who maintained the original Hebrew of Hebrew Scripture, as evidenced by the Dead Sea Scrolls. But since the overwhelming majority of the people spoke Aramaic, something needed to be done to ensure that rabbis and scribes could read from Scripture during the Sabbath in a language that people would understand. Scholars therefore believe that in Jesus' day, there would have been several Aramaic translations of the Bible in circulation, known as *Targumim* (the plural of Targum). One such Targum, an Aramaic translation of the Book of Job, is mentioned in reference to Rabbi Gamaliel I, a contemporary of Jesus. A Targum of Job also forms part of the Dead Sea Scrolls, dating to the first century BCE.[1] Jesus' familiarity with such Targumim is suggested by the Gospels, who as we saw previously, quote him crying out a verse from Psalm 22, in Aramaic, during his last moments on the cross: *Eloi, Eloi, lema sabachthani?* "My God, my God, why have you forsaken me?" (Mark 15:34).[2]

This being the case, would Jesus, in formulating his prayer, have debts in mind, or sins? The case of debt is supported by the fact that as we saw, many Galilean peasants were deeply indebted to their tax collectors. The parable of the Talents and Pounds (Matthew 25:14–30), the Creditor (Luke 7:41–43), and many others all illustrate the erosive impact of debt on Galilean society. The heavy tax burden Herod and his successors placed on farmers in Galilee forced these people to borrow heavily, so as to satisfy the tax collector. Debt, in other words, was a daily source of concern for most Galileans, if not an existential threat. What Matthew's version seems to say is that we should share this burden equally, and that in the Kingdom of God, we should be willing to forgive our debtors as readily as we would expect debt relief from others. Some scholars have tried to relate Matthew's "forgiveness of debts" to the year of Jubilee, or the Sabbatical year, when according to Leviticus all debts were to be cancelled, all forfeited lands returned and all slaves freed (Leviticus 25:8–12). The problem with this interpretation is that the Jubilee and Sabbatical years may have been observed in the kingdoms of ancient Israel, but most likely not in the Roman Palestine of Jesus' time, subject to Roman rule and law.

Most modern Christian denominations take their cue from Luke, who interprets the verse in a moral sense, as *sins*. In that sense, the prayer acknowledges that as human beings we are bound to be fallible, and therefore prone to mistakes or *trespasses*. We are sinners, all of us, and only God is able to forgive the sins we have committed. But Luke's version suggests that in the Kingdom of God, this requires reciprocity. In other words, if we expect God to be merciful toward us, then we have the moral duty to extend that same mercy and forgiveness to those who may have done us wrong. As Jesus says in Matthew, "For if you forgive others their trespasses, your heavenly Father will also forgive you, but if you do not forgive others, neither will your Father forgive your trespasses" (Matthew 6:14–15).

This has a special resonance for us today, because in our modern times, mercy and tolerance are endangered virtues. Even though the twenty-first century has made so many advances in terms of technology and economic development, it seems that as a human species we have regressed in our tolerance toward one another. Some have seized on that phenomenon to quite deliberately divide us, by projecting our grievances on a certain class of people who are different from us in race, orientation, or outlook. That is not a new phenomenon, for the idea of identifying a scapegoat in society as the target for individual grievance is as old as the hills. Emperor Nero blamed the Christians in Rome for the Great Fire of 64 CE that devastated large parts of the city. For centuries, Christians in Europe reserved a special animus toward Jews. The Fourth Lateran Council, convoked by Pope Innocent III in 1216 and attended by nearly five hundred bishops and patriarchs, decreed that Jews and Muslims living in Christian lands must "wear a special dress to enable them to be distinguished from Christians." The canon set in motion a process that would increasingly marginalize Jews in Europe, culminating in the creation of ghettos in the sixteenth century and pogroms of the nineteenth century. As many historians have suggested, this antisemitism became the justification for the infamous Nazi Final Solution in the 1930s and 1940s.

Jesus' prayer tells us that there is no room for prejudice and hate in the Kingdom of God. To be a Christian, Jesus tells us, we must ban every form of envy, intolerance and hatred from our heart. That is sometimes difficult, because it is much easier to blame others for things we don't like, or things we would like to have but can't get.

Forgive us our trespasses, as we forgive others. That is the essential touchstone of Jesus' call for compassion and love in the Kingdom of God.

9

DO NOT BRING US TO THE TEST

The meaning of the last verse of the Lucan *Our Father,* *wǝ-La taʿel lan lǝ-nisyon,* has likewise led to many debates in the scholarly community. What is this test, this *peirasmos* to use Luke's term, that Jesus is talking about? Why would a merciful God want to lead us to temptation? Why would he want to test our faith? One answer is that as humans, we are fallible and must often be reminded of the innate benevolence of God, particularly in moments of great distress. A perfect example is the story of Abraham and Isaac. God told Abraham, "take your son, your only son Isaac, whom you love, and go to the land of Moriah, and offer him there as a burnt offering on one of the mountains that I shall show you" (Genesis 22:2). With a heavy heart, Abraham complied, but just before he struck the blade to kill his son, an angel intervened. Relieved beyond words, Abraham offered a ram instead. Similar tests are visited on the people of Israel during their long sojourn in the desert (Exodus 16:4; 20:20) and even on Jesus himself, who is tempted by the devil in the wilderness (Mark 1:12). In the view of John Yieh, the verse is reassuring in "that, even if God may sometimes lead us in temptation, God is faithful and will not let us be 'tempted' beyond our strength but will always provide a way out so that we may be able to endure it."[1]

Another view holds that "test" refers to the great apocalypse, a colossal battle between good and evil that, according to many apocalyptic visions in the Second Temple period, would herald the Kingdom of God at the End Times, the day of Last Judgment. Based on the Gospel accounts, it is likely that John the Baptist was one of those who warned of a great conflagration on the horizon. This has prompted some historians to argue that John the Baptist may have been a member of the Qumran sect, the community that hid the Dead Sea Scrolls in nearby caves. The evidence for this suggestion are a number of parallels between the words of the Baptist and what we know about the Qumranites.[2] According to one of the Qumran sectarian documents, the mission of the sect was to prepare for the final struggle between the forces of good and evil, between "Darkness" and "Light" while anticipating the arrival of the Messiah, "the Prince of Light." The documents suggest that the members of this community were educated scribes, sages, or even Zadokite priests who wished to live in the desert, far removed from Judea's increasingly Hellenistic urban culture. Other texts also instruct each member that "his property and his possessions shall be given to the hand of the man who is the examiner over the possessions of the many." Similarly, John the Baptist told his audience that "Whoever has two coats must share with anyone who has none; and whoever has food must do likewise" (Luke 3:10–11). And lastly, the Qumranites practiced ritual immersion in their baths, their *mikva'ot*, which archaeologists led by Roland de Vaux excavated in the 1950s. John baptized his followers in the flowing waters of the Jordan River.

John, too, saw the coming of the Messiah as part of a violent regime change and warned his audience that "even now the ax is lying at the root of the trees; every tree therefore that does not bear good fruit is cut down and thrown into the fire" (Luke 3:9). John's militant language about a coming cataclysm would suggest that he saw the *Mashiach* in a military sense, one who would reconquer the Jewish nation through force of arms. Some scholars see a parallel with the Book of Revelation, which uses the same Greek word for test, *peirasmos,* as "trial": "Because you have kept my word about patient endurance, I will keep you from the hour of trial that is coming on the whole world" (Revelation 3:10). From the perspective of Revelation, therefore, *Lead us not to the test* could be a petition to God to save the faithful from the horrors of the Last Judgment and allow the righteous to enter the Kingdom on the strength of their faith.

Another view is that *test* or *trial* refers to the misfortunes that all of us, as human beings, will encounter as part of our lives. We may be disappointed in not getting the job we so desperately want, or fail to get the promotion we thought we deserved. On a more serious note, we may be tested through the illness or even the death of a loved one. There is nothing more tragic, for example, than having a child in our circle of family or friends succumb to an illness or an accident. We often ask ourselves, why would God permit such a thing? Why does he test us so much? The Letter of James, possibly attributed to Jesus' brother, has an answer for that question. He writes, "My brothers and sisters, whenever you face trials of any kind, consider it nothing but joy, because you know that the testing of your faith produces endurance; and let endurance have its full effect, so that you may be mature and complete, lacking in nothing" (James 1:2–4). And Paul reminds us that "No trial has overtaken you that is not faced by others. And God is faithful: He will not let you be tried beyond what you are able to bear, but with the trial will also provide a way out so that you may be able to endure it" (1 Corinthians 10:13). In other words, God's purpose in allowing trials in our lives is to make us stronger and more faithful.

In our modern day, we have experienced many tests ourselves. Paramount among these was the Great Pandemic of COVID-19, which at the time of this writing, has infected 642 million people worldwide, causing 6.63 million deaths. Climate change poses a huge test to humankind, bringing the threat of more frequent droughts, heat waves, rising sea levels, melting glaciers, and warming oceans, endangering our food supply and human habitats.

Still, most Christian communities today prefer the translation *Do not lead us into temptation,* in part because Jesus himself referred to temptation as a human failing, a weakness that prevents us from doing what is right. Throughout his ministry, Jesus often found that his followers, simple fishermen for the most part, could not summon either the courage or the commitment to actively support what Jesus was trying to accomplish. Part of the reason for this is that throughout the Gospel stories, the Apostles are often left clueless about what it is that Jesus is talking about. "Do you not yet understand?" an exasperated Jesus tells them at one point, before launching into another parable (Mark 8:21). "Then how will you understand all the parables?"

Another scene in which the Apostles let Jesus down occurs after the Last Supper when Jesus leads his followers out of Jerusalem under cover of darkness. It had been a harrowing day; during their visit to the Temple, when Jesus was hoping to deliver his great sermon to the crowds who had gathered for Passover, they were thwarted by the fact that the Temple forecourt had been converted into a noisy bazaar, filled with stalls for paschal lambs and moneychangers. Passover was a time when every head of a household had to offer a lamb or a goat for sacrifice by the priests, but the animal had to be free from blemish (Exodus 12:5). But year after year, pilgrims had found that trying to get their lamb through the crowds and the narrow streets of Jerusalem without it being shoved and scratched was nearly impossible.[3]

Unbeknownst to Jesus, the high priest Caiaphas had decided to bring the sale of such lambs inside the Temple walls, in the large Herodian forecourt. This way, pilgrims could buy their lamb, sanctioned by the priesthood, and take it straight through the Court of Women and into the Court of Priests, where the altar stood and the animals were butchered. But this had raised another problem. Inside the Temple only one form of currency could be used: the Tyrian Shekel. So if someone happened to have currency such as Roman sesterces or Greek drachmae, which was the case for most worshippers, those coins had to be changed into shekels at the prevailing rate.

It may have been a good idea, but in practice the whole thing devolved into chaos. All sense of order in the Temple was lost as hundreds of pilgrims pushed, shoved, screamed, and begged to get their money changed and to purchase a lamb before the supply ran out. Jesus was devastated; his moment to deliver his great sermon was slipping away from him. And so he "began to drive out those who were selling and those who were buying in the temple, and he overturned the tables of the money changers" (Mark 11:15).

From that moment, Jesus became a marked man. A warrant went out to the Temple Guards for his arrest. That is the reason why Jesus and his disciples could not return to

| *The Tyrian Shekel, the only currency allowed in the Temple.*

Bethany for the Seder, because it was still daylight and the city gates were heavily guarded. Instead, as we saw, they had to improvise and find a venue at the last moment where the group could celebrate this holy meal. They found a place in the city, but when the meal was served, it turned out that one of the Apostles, a man named Judas, had succumbed to the oldest temptation: the lure of money. He had secretly gone to the chief priests, who no doubt were waiting for news of Jesus' arrest, and asked them, "What will you give me if I betray him to you?" The chief priests replied, "thirty pieces of silver" (Matthew 26:14–15).

We can imagine why. The chief priests would have known that the chances of catching Jesus in a city teeming with thousands of strangers—including many Galileans—would have been almost impossible. The offer of one of Jesus' followers to lead the Guards to Jesus' hideout would have been welcomed with open arms. With this information, the priests could recall their roving patrols and concentrate their forces on the area where Jesus was believed to be later that night. Perhaps Judas even knew that later in the evening, the group was going to attempt a breakout toward the east, to the Mount of Olives.

Many scholars are inclined to accept the story of Judas, based on the so-called criterion of embarrassment. There is no way to cast the betrayal by one of Jesus' closest companions in a favorable light. It must have been one of those historical events that were too well known for the evangelists to ignore. Moreover, the theme of the Apostles failing Jesus is a key element of Mark's Gospel. In the view of this evangelist, the disciples are dim-witted; they don't understand what Jesus is talking about; they fret and complain, or fight amongst themselves about who is the best and the brightest. In this, they are not unlike the Israelites in the desert, who try Moses' patience with their tireless whining and their weak faith in God.

But was Judas' betrayal truly motivated by temptation? In the 1970s, a leather-bound manuscript was discovered near Beni Masar in Egypt. Written in Coptic, the text eventually became known as the Codex Tchacos and was finally published in English as the "Judas Gospel" by the National Geographic Society in 2006. The text argues that Judas acted according to Jesus' own instructions. According to this document, Jesus knew that he had to suffer and die in order to fulfill what was foretold in the Scriptures. He merely relied on Judas to expedite his arrest and execution. Far from being a traitor, then, Judas was a deeply loyal and obedient follower who performed Jesus' order to the letter, notwithstanding his deep sorrow.

The problem is that this document originated much later than the canonical Gospels, Q, or Thomas, or the Gospel of Peter. As we have seen, there were many Christian sects and movements in the second and third centuries CE that broke away from the traditional doctrine originally formulated by Paul. These movements sought to bolster their authority by writing "Gospels" ascribed (pseudonymously) to notable figures

The first page of the Gospel of Judas (page 33 of the Codex Tchacos).

in Jesus' immediate circle. The sect that produced the Gospel of Judas, for reasons not fully understood, specifically sought to exculpate Judas—the disciple who betrayed Jesus. The Gospel text may, in fact, reveal the hand of a Gnostic author from the late second century CE for whom Jesus was a divine being through and through. Seen from his perspective, the "betrayal" was actually an act of mercy that released Jesus from his corporeal bonds and restored him as a divine being.

Modern scholarship, however, has rejected the validity of this claim. They point out that Judas was known as Judas Iscariot (Mark 3:19; Matthew 10:4). The term *Iskariot* has often been linked to the name *sicarius,* Latin for "daggerman," an epithet associated with the Jewish party of the Zealots. This was a movement prompted by the Quirinius census of 6 CE, who opposed paying taxes to the Romans on religious principles: the land belonged to God, not to Rome. Many decades later, in the 50s CE, they would begin to form a militia that ultimately launched the First Jewish Revolt in 66 CE. But in Jesus' time, they were largely known for their strict piety. There was, in fact, a "declared" member of the Zealots among Jesus' followers, known as Simon the Zealot (Luke 6:15; Acts 1:13). However, when the evangelists wrote their Gospels in the latter part of the first century, many Jewish Christians outside of Judea felt that the Jewish Revolt was a catastrophe and that the Zealots were terrorists rather than resistance fighters. Judas would have fit that picture nicely.

But there may be another explanation for Judas' name. *Iskariot* may simply mean that Judas was a man (*Ish*) from *Kerioth,* a town in southern Judea. This is important, for that would make Judas the only non-Galilean in Jesus' inner circle. Given what we know about the Judean prejudice against Galileans, Judas may have felt that as a native Judean, he was best qualified to find a way out of the impasse now facing the group—by entering into direct, face-to-face negotiations with the Temple authorities. By striking a deal by which Jesus, and *only* Jesus, would be taken into custody and the rest would be allowed to go free, Judas may have thought that he had made the best of an otherwise hopeless situation.

In fact, by giving Jesus an honest opportunity to make his case, in front of the full college of the Sanhedrin, Judas may have thought he was, indeed, acting in Jesus' best interests. After all, that was the reason Jesus had traveled to Jerusalem to begin with: to address the religious leaders and citizens of Jerusalem. It was a lot better than being on the run as a fugitive, at the risk of being cut down at any moment by a Guardsman. That Judas had the full confidence of Jesus, and therefore enjoyed a close relationship with him, is suggested by John's claim that Judas was entrusted with the group's "money-box" (John 12:6). In other words, if Jesus did choose Judas as the movement's treasurer, he must have trusted the man as an honest and reliable companion.

The next great disappointment awaited Jesus after he led his disciples to a favored spot on the Mount of Olives, known as Gethsemane. The name is derived from the Aramaic *Gaḏ-Šmānê*, or *Gat-Shemanim* in Hebrew, which means "oil press." Oil presses were usually set up in caves so that the pressing of olives could take place in a cool environment, out of the hot sun. In the winter months, the cave would have been empty and well suited for a place of refuge.

Jesus hoped that his followers would stay with him and offer him succor in these tense and dangerous hours, particularly because the Mount of Olives would have been teeming with thousands of pilgrims and their families, camping out in the open; the hostels and inns in the city were too expensive. Few of these people would have been able to afford a paschal lamb; instead, they would have scraped together enough pennies to buy a dove, and they would now be filling their bellies with vegetable stew, scooped out of the communal pot with a piece of hardtack *matzo*.

| *A cave on the Mount of Olives, traditionally identified with Gethsemane.*

As Luke says, "When he reached the place, he said to them, "Pray that you may not come into the time of trial" (Luke 22:40). The word that Luke uses for "trial," *peirasmos,* is the same word he uses for the verse "do not bring us to the *test.*" But it was to no avail. As Jesus got up from prayer, says Luke, "he came to the disciples and found them sleeping because of grief, and he said to them, 'Why are you sleeping? Get up and pray that you may not come into the time of trial'" (Luke 22:45–46).

All of these references lead me to conclude that in the Lord's Prayer, Jesus is indeed talking about temptation: the temptation of giving in to indolence, to passivity, of not doing anything to help build the Kingdom of God. It is often much easier to look the other way when we encounter someone who is in need of our help.

In fact, Jesus told a parable about exactly that type of passive behavior, in the famous story of the Good Samaritan. A Jewish man, says Luke, "was going down from Jerusalem to Jericho" when he "fell into the hands of robbers, who stripped him, beat him, and went away, leaving him half dead" (Luke 10:30). It so happened that shortly after this attack, two people passed the victim: a priest and a Levite. They both tried hard to ignore the unfortunate man and refused to come to his aid. But then, a Samaritan passed by. Most Jews in Jesus' time avoided contact with Samaritans, who were the inhabitants of the region called Samaria, for their race and bloodlines were believed to have been contaminated by intermarriage with Babylonian settlers. And yet, it was the Samaritan who took pity on the man. He "bandaged his wounds, having poured oil and wine on them," and then took him to an inn, where he gave the innkeeper two denarii (about forty U.S. dollars) for the victim's care (Luke 10:30–37). The parable is meant to illustrate two key tenets of the Kingdom: compassion for one's fellow human being, and the utter rejection of racial prejudice. In fact, Jesus is prompted to tell the story by a lawyer, who asks him what he must do to inherit eternal life. Jesus answers by referring the lawyer to the Torah, which commands one to "love the Lord your God, and to love your neighbor as yourself" (Deuteronomy 6:5; Leviticus 19:18). For Jesus, "there is no other commandment greater than these," emphasizing selfless love as the cardinal pillar of the Kingdom (Mark 12:28–31).

That is the essential takeaway of the verse *And do not lead us into temptation*: that we must never feel tempted to place our own needs and survival above those who are near to us. In this interpretation, the verse asks God for strength to resist any form of temptation of a material or physical nature that will deter us from doing good. "Each person is tempted when he is lured and enticed by his own desire," says the Letter of James, and that is as valid today as it was in Jesus' time (James 1:14).

10

DELIVER US FROM EVIL

From the outset we have been guided by Luke's version of the Lord's Prayer, but we cannot conclude our story without also taking into consideration Matthew's great coda, *And deliver us from evil* (Matthew 6:13). The NRSV translation hews closely to the Greek version: "but rescue us from the evil one" (*ponērou*). The word πονηρός or *Ponēros* is an adjective that means evil or wicked, but as in the case of the English use of "evil," it can also be used as a noun. The same word also appears in Matthew's parable of the "wicked man" who put weeds among the grain, so that when the grain stalks grew to full height, they were surrounded by weeds. And, Matthew says, Jesus explained the parable by saying, "The one who sows the good seed is the Son of Man; the field is the world, and the good seed are the children of the kingdom; the weeds are the children of the evil one, and the enemy who sowed them is the devil; the harvest is the end of the age, and the reapers are angels" (Matthew 13:37–39).

This segment makes it clear that Jesus is talking about Satan, the personification of human evil. Satan and his acolytes, the demons, appear frequently in the Gospel stories because they represent the exact opposite of what the Kingdom is about: a world ruled by selfishness, lust, and base desires. According to Luke and John, it was Satan who urged Judas to betray Jesus in return for thirty pieces of silver (Luke 22:3–4; John 13:27). But what evil, specifically, is meant in Matthew's last verse? Whom did the people of Galilee and Judea believe to be the henchmen of Satan? For the peasants of Galilee, the answer was clear: the Herodian dynasty and its collaborators, the tax collectors and the landowners, who had confiscated the land of the peasantry and condemned them to a life of penury. For the people of Judea, however, the answer may have been more nuanced.

The fact of the matter is that for more than a century now, ancient Israel had been a deeply polarized nation, with grave tensions roiling just beneath the surface—as in our own world today. The Maccabean Revolt, led by the brothers of the Maccabeus family from 166 BCE onward, had succeeded in 142 BCE to wrest control of Judea from the Syrian dynasty of Seleucid kings, but its independence came at a price. In 150 BCE, Jonathan Maccabeus combined the position of king with that of the Jewish high priest, the *Kohen Gadol,* a title of great religious and political significance. The high priest of Israel was the supreme steward of the sacrificial cult at the Temple, and the ultimate authority for the forgiveness of sins through animal sacrifice. By usurping this sacred position, Jonathan and subsequent Hasmonean kings exerted full control over both the political and religious spheres of their nation, but it outraged many pious Jews. They held steadfast to the rule that only descendants of Aaron, the brother of Moses, through Solomon's priest Zadok could qualify to serve as high priest.

The result was a catastrophic disintegration of the Jewish nation—between those who consented to the Hasmonean absorption of the position of high priest, and those who fought it tooth and nail. Imagine, for example, the outcry if today the Italian prime minister would also forcibly assume the throne of St. Peter and become the pontiff of the Catholic Church! A further point of contention was that the Hasmonean kings increasingly adopted a Greek (and therefore pagan) lifestyle, which was seen by many *Hasidim* ("pious" or "wise ones" in the books of Daniel and 1 Maccabees) as an evil cancer at the heart of the Judean nation.

All this was cause for great conflict within the nation of Israel because the priesthood had always served as an important unifying body. Even during the days of King Cyrus the Great, when Judea formed part of the Persian Empire, a priestly elite had governed the province as a *de facto* autonomous government. And during the subsequent Ptolemaic and Seleucid occupation, the colonial governors had gladly deferred the adjudication of civil matters and minor crimes to the priesthood, specifically the Council of the Great Sanhedrin, which had jurisdiction over both religious and domestic matters. Control over the Sanhedrin was shared by two parties: the Sadducees on the one hand, and the predominantly lay brotherhood known as the Pharisees on the other.

Both these parties often make their appearance in the Gospels (for example, Matthew 3:7). The Sadducees (or *Tzedoqim* in Hebrew) formed the aristocratic upper crust of Jewish society. Deeply conservative, they controlled the elaborate apparatus of ritual sacrifice at the Second Temple, including the collection

A reconstruction of the Stoa of the Temple, which contained the Chamber of Hewn Stones, the seat of the Great Sanhedrin.

of tithes from every Jew in Judea and throughout the Diaspora. The Sadducees did not accept any Scripture beyond the Torah—including the Books of the Prophets—and rejected any idea of an afterlife or the immortality of the soul. They also exerted real secular power. During the Hasmonean Era, the Sadducees were given majority control of the Sanhedrin as well as the administration of the Temple, in return for Sadducee support of the Hasmonean regime, including its double role of king and high priest. After the Roman takeover, they then eagerly collaborated with King Herod, who likewise agreed to grant them full control of the Temple operations and its lucrative collection of tithes.

Of course, this did not sit well with the principal opposition to the Sadducees, namely the Pharisaic party. As we saw previously, the Pharisees (derived from the Hebrew *perushim,* or "separated ones") were a group composed of both priests and pious laymen who were passionately devoted to the application of the Jewish Law in everyday life, rather than just within the Temple precinct. The Pharisees strenuously opposed the militaristic and Hellenistic tendencies of the Hasmonean rulers and objected to Sadducee control of the Temple. The reason is that the Pharisees felt that Jews should please God in everything they did, and not just think they could find forgiveness for their sins by making an animal sacrifice. The Pharisaic concern for purity, so often maligned in the Gospels, was actually an attempt to transfer the priestly rules governing purity from the Temple to everyone's home, thus diluting the influence of the Sadducees and make every Jew an active participant in the worship of *Adonai*, "the Lord." Whereas the Sadducees considered the written texts of the Torah a closed book, the Pharisees continued to debate and interpret the application of the Jewish Law to everyday life—a corpus of wisdom and exegesis that, as we saw, became known as the Oral Law. The Pharisees also accepted the idea of the immortality of the soul, as well as the belief in the resurrection after Judgment Day—two concepts that would return in the teachings of Jesus. Socially, too, the Pharisees were different from the wealthy Sadducee aristocracy. In a sense they were a professional "middle class" of scribes, teachers, tradesmen, and craftsmen (Mark 2:16). For them, the idea of debating and adapting the Torah to the changing conditions of everyday life was the very essence of being a Pharisee.

The Gospels often lump the Pharisees together with the Sadducees as the principal antagonists of Jesus (Matthew 16:1). We must remind ourselves that when the evangelists wrote their story, based on prevailing oral and written traditions, the Sadducees and the Temple had ceased to exist. Many scholars believe that it was the Pharisees who survived the upheaval of the

First Jewish War of 66–70 CE and subsequently lay the ground-work for a new form of Judaism, *rabbinic* Judaism. This tradition was no longer based on animal sacrifice but on the study of Hebrew Scripture—thus continuing the Oral Law debates of decades past. The evangelists, who lived outside of Roman Palestine, may not have had this information and were therefore unable to clearly distinguish between the two groups. As a result, I believe that the evangelists misunderstand the reports of fierce debates between Jesus and the Pharisees. The truth of the matter is, both had much in common. That's why Pharisees sought out Jesus and engaged him in discussion, not because they rejected him but because they were intrigued by his ideas. They might not always agree with him, but they believed his ideas had merit, otherwise they would not have bothered with a humble *hasid* from Galilee. Like the Jesus movement itself, the Pharisees were in many ways a minority party of progressives, people who clamored for change against the stifling grip of the Romans and their collaborators, the Sadducees. In fact, the Gospels admit that many Pharisees openly sympathized with the Jesus movement. When Herod Antipas heard about the success of Jesus' preaching and sought to arrest him, it was the Pharisees who warned him to get away (Luke 13:31). And after Jesus was crucified, it was two prominent Pharisees, Nicodemus (John 3:1–15) and Joseph of Arimathea (Mark 15:42–47), both members of the Sanhedrin, who assisted in Jesus' burial.

The Sadducees and the Pharisees were not the only factions in Jesus' time. One group, called the Essenes by Josephus, formed a "commune" of sorts to pursue an ascetic lifestyle entirely based on the Torah, the Law. These Essenes were likewise outraged by the Hasmonean usurpation of the office of high priest.[1] Living in monastic retreats, the Essenes dressed in simple robes, prayed at regular intervals, and worked long hours tilling the soil. "They despise riches," Josephus wrote, claiming that the movement numbered around four thousand members, "and it is a law among them, that those who join must let whatever they have be shared with the whole order." Many scholars have argued that the community of Qumran, which hid the Dead Sea Scrolls in nearby caves, may have been an offshoot of the Essenes, though this issue continues to be debated.

The "fourth philosophy" during the early years of the Roman occupation was a group known as the Zealots. As we saw in previous chapters, these people were incensed by the famous census of Quirinius of 6 CE, which took place after Judea was annexed as a Crown Province by Emperor Augustus, and the question arose what this province was worth in terms of tax receipts. This led to another revolt—the second rebellion in Jesus' lifetime—led by a man called Judas the Galilean.[2] The Roman census, Judas claimed, was illegal because the land to be assessed did not belong to Rome but to God. It was God who

The settlement of Qumran near the Dead Sea, believed by some to have belonged to an offshoot of the Essenes.

had given the Promised Land to his people, for them to till as tenants. To submit to the census and accept the Roman occupation as a fait accompli was therefore tantamount to accepting the yoke of slavery and rejecting the Lord's title to his property. Consequently, Judas urged the populace to simply refuse any dealings with the Roman authorities, at any level, whether involving the census or any other form of contact. Josephus presents this Judas movement as an outlaw force simply by virtue of their opposition to the Romans, as is his habit. Yet it is far from clear whether the Judas movement in Jesus' day was indeed an active resistance force or merely a civil-disobedience movement. Nowhere do we hear about this Judas actually instigating attacks on Roman patrols, as Judas, son of Hezekiah had done a decade earlier, or in any other way resorting to violence to realize his goals. He may have done what Gandhi did in pre- and postwar India—paralyze the foreign administration by organizing widespread nonviolent resistance.[3]

Of course, history is written by victors. In this case, the history of Roman Palestine in the first half of the first century CE was written by Josephus, a man writing for the Romans on behalf of a Roman sponsor, the Flavian House of Emperor Vespasian. As a result, Josephus' story is almost exclusively preoccupied with the actions of the powerful elites who ruled the territory during the years of Jesus' life. The peasants and dayworkers who made up the vast majority of Galilee's population rarely figure in his narrative; and when they do appear on his radar, it is usually as a group of "bandits" or "outlaws" who decide to terrorize the citizenry and challenge the sovereignty of Rome.

It is not surprising, therefore, that Josephus rarely bothers to ask himself *why* the peasants of Galilee would be involved in not one, but several desperate revolts against the ruling regime in the span of a mere ten years. The fact is that Josephus couldn't have cared less about the fate of the Jewish peasantry. As a member of a priestly aristocratic family, raised in a world of privilege, Josephus looked upon the world as one inevitably divided between the haves and the have-nots.

There were other sources of evil in Jesus' lifetime, and one was quite simply, disease. As we saw, disease in Galilee had become rampant when many peasants were forced off their land and no longer had the ability to feed themselves and their families with basic nutrition. One form of chronic illness that occurs most frequently in the Gospels, with nine references, is "leprosy" ('sara'at). Modern research has shown that this disease is not what medical science today has identified as leprosy or Hansen's disease. Hansen's disease is an infectious condition caused by an organism called *Mycobacterium leprae* that produces disfiguring skin lesions, nerve damage, and progressive debility. Paleopathologists have found only limited evidence of this disease in skeletons from ancient Israel. By contrast, scientists believe, based on the description of leprosy in the Book of Leviticus, that the Bible is talking about a wide range of skin diseases (such as psoriasis), which in Israel were regarded as ritually unclean. We may therefore assume that the Gospels use the term "leprosy" for any chronic or parasitic disease with skin manifestations such as discoloration, scarring, or swelling of the skin. Some historians have argued that the New Testament form of leprosy refers to a particularly virulent form of nonvenereal syphilis, transmitted not through sexual intercourse but by skin contact, mostly in childhood.[4]

My point is, however, that Jesus' contemporaries would not have understood the medical reasons underlying these conditions. In contrast, disease was often ascribed to the work of the evil incarnate: Satan or his acolytes, the demons. For example, after Jesus formally launches his ministry in the synagogue of Capernaum and heals Simon Peter's mother-in-law, who was in bed with a fever, "the whole city" gathered at the door, and "he cured many who were sick with various diseases, and cast out many demons" (Mark 1:34). Shortly thereafter, says Mark, "he went throughout Galilee, proclaiming the message in their synagogues and casting out demons" (Mark 1:39). One of these was a leper who begged Jesus, "If you choose, you can make me clean." Moved with pity, Mark continues, Jesus "stretched out his hand and touched him, and said to him, 'I do choose. Be made clean!' Immediately the leprosy left him, and he was made clean" (Mark 1:40–42). Jesus urged him to stay quiet about this and only show himself to a priest, in order to be certified as ritually pure, but of course the man was so ecstatic that he ran around and spread the word. In no time, says Mark, "people came to [Jesus] from every quarter" (Mark 1:45).

From a purely theological perspective, the meaning of this healing story and the many other healing miracles in the Gospels is to signify that Jesus has the power to defeat Satan, to defeat evil, and to forcibly remove demonic beings from the body of the sick. Josephus claims that it was only through a miraculous sign (*sēmeion*) such as a healing or an exorcism that a prophet could prove he was truly speaking with the voice of God: that his teachings were divinely inspired. "The ability to [exorcise] remains very strong among us even to this day," Josephus writes, and adds that he once witnessed an exorcism performed by a Jew named Eleazar.[5] Miracles, therefore, were seen as a seal of divine approval. Those unable to work miracles or pull off amazing deeds were, by default, branded as false prophets.

This has prompted some scholars to dismiss the healing miracles in the Gospels as the product of pious imagination in the oral traditions about Jesus. Some believe we should look for a symbolic rather than an actual physical meaning of the miracle stories. Rudolf Bultmann, for example, argued that the early Church celebrated the miraculous conversion of water into wine in Cana on January 6—the Feast of the Epiphany. In Antiquity, this date was associated with the feast of Dionysus, when empty jars at every temple and shrine dedicated to the god were filled with wine. Bultmann believes that the Cana story was meant as a message to John's Hellenistic audience that Dionysus had been upstaged by a far more powerful deity, namely Jesus, the Son of God.[6]

That may be true, but I strongly believe that the healing stories cannot be so easily dismissed. Even in the earliest oral strata, such as Q, Jesus has always been closely identified with a remarkable ability to heal. John Meier, author of a series of books on the historical Jesus, has tried to make some sense about the miracle traditions by making a careful distinction between the so-called *healing* miracles and *nature* miracles in the Gospels. Nature miracles include such phenomena as the feeding of the five thousand, the stilling of the storm, the change of water into wine, and Jesus' ability to walk on water. Meier argued that unlike the healing stories, which follow a predictable vocabulary and literary form, the nature miracles have no recognizable pattern.[7] Furthermore, nature miracles have fewer multiple attestations. The story of the miraculous catch of fish, for example, occurs only in Luke, and the story of the miraculous conversion of water into wine at Cana appears only in John. Many scholars are therefore inclined to ascribe the nature miracles to the enthusiastic imagination of oral transmission and a desire to underscore the unprecedented nature of Jesus, lest the message somehow be lost on future generations.

The healing miracles, on the other hand, are consistently reported across all three Synoptic Gospels, as well as, in some cases, the Gospel of John. We must therefore conclude that Jesus' ability to heal is an authentic attribute in the oldest sources about Jesus. Naturally, for Christians, Jesus' healing powers are accepted as a matter of faith. From a purely historical viewpoint, however, we could ask if it is possible to explain these supernatural powers with the modern scientific tools at our disposal. If Jesus truly had the ability to heal the sick, how did he do that? And does the Gospel material provide us with enough diagnostic information to verify the healing procedures attributed to Jesus?

Lots of ink has been spilled on this issue, but as I described in my book *In the Footsteps of Jesus,* it is remarkable that Jesus often begins his healing with the phrase "Your sins are forgiven" (Mark 2.5). For us, this sounds rather odd. It is nice to know that one's sins are forgiven, but what does this have to do with disease? The Bible provides the answer. As we saw earlier, in ancient Israel illness and disease were routinely regarded as God's punishment for sins. As God says in the Book of Exodus, "for I the Lord your God am a jealous God, punishing children for the transgressions of parents, to the third and fourth generation" (Exodus 20:5 and 34:7; also Psalm 109:13–14). Because disease was considered a mark of sin and evil, the chronically ill were often forced to live in squalor on the periphery of the village. In other words, the strain of chronic illness was compounded by the emotional stress of being excluded from the culture and comforts of the village.

That is why Jesus begins his healing by telling his patients that they are no longer sinners, and that they deserve the same human dignity of those who are healthy. This is immediately followed up by another form of intervention, in which Jesus asks, "Do you have faith?" This has an important psychological bearing. Jesus is asking whether the patient has faith in his ability to heal him (Luke 7:50). In other words, the patient must have the sheer *will* to get better. It's not that different from when our doctors tell us, "Take this, and it will make you feel better." That expectation is a key element of our recovery.

But we can't just dismiss the healing stories as simply the result of the so-called "placebo effect," the power of suggestion, as some scholars have done. And that brings us to the third element of Jesus' healing strategy: his touch. Jesus makes a point of touching or embracing the ill, thus rejecting the prevailing notion that the diseased were unclean. For someone bereft of human intimacy for years, the physical touch of Jesus must have been an incredible experience. Jesus' deliberate proximity to the patient, his assurance that any presumed sins are null and void, and the comfort of a physical embrace all amount to powerful stimuli to the natural healing process. Today, modern medicine acknowledges that the brain plays the greatest role in a person's health and recovery. Some specialists believe that 40 percent of the human healing process is physical, but 60 percent is driven by mental factors.

But even that doesn't tell the full story. In addition to these comforting words, Jesus must have had a special ability to improve the condition of the sufferers who were brought to him. Some years ago, I made a study of Eastern medicine for a documentary series titled *Miraculous Health* that aired on Public

Television and international networks. I was particularly interested in the effects of electromagnetic energy on the healing process. For anyone with some familiarity with Eastern medicine, spanning a practice of three thousand years, this will come as no surprise. Both the Ayurvedic philosophy of the chakras and the Chinese concept of *qi* point to energy concentrations in the human body. What's more, these traditions acknowledge that there are certain practitioners with the gift of actually manipulating the electromagnetic energy field of a human being. During the production of this television series, we had the opportunity to observe this electromagnetic healing (EMH) in therapy, by filming the practice of Dr. Rick Levy, a clinical psychologist with five board certifications in his field. The results were astonishing. By repeatedly moving his hands in close proximity to specific areas of pain or disease (thus directing concentrated waves of energy into the patient's body), Dr. Levy was able to alleviate anywhere from sixty to one hundred percent of the pain sensations reported by the patient. In one such session, a woman suffering from debilitating back pain was able to stand up straight, free of pain, for the first time in thirty years.

Dr. Levy is hardly an exception. Today, there are a number of clinicians and biofield practitioners who can see and actually intervene in a patient's aura or biofield. Many believe that this aura is composed of seven layers, whereby the inner layers represent the physical and emotional functioning of the body, while the outer layers (extending two to three feet from the body), serve to establish harmony with the surrounding world.[8]

I believe that there is at least a possibility that Jesus was endowed with the gift of electromagnetic healing, and that he only became aware of this gift when confronted with the epidemic incidence of disease during his travels as a young rabbi through

Lower Galilee. The people around him may have intuitively felt the unique power of his magnetic presence. Mark describes a situation where, unbeknownst to Jesus, a woman who had been suffering from hemorrhages for twelve years moved up behind him to touch his cloak. She thought, "If I but touch his cloak, I will be made well." Indeed, her hemorrhaging stopped. Mark reports that Jesus was immediately aware "that power had gone from him." Significantly, this healing is reported in all three Synoptic Gospels (Mark 5:25–30; Matthew 9:18–26; Luke 8:40–56).

There is no precedent for this form of healing in either the Old or New Testament. Other healing episodes are invariably the result of a prophet consciously praying or invoking the power of God to bring a miraculous event about. The idea that healing could take place through physical touch between two human beings and the resulting transfer of energy is simply without precedent. For Jesus, this would have affirmed his ability to defeat Satan by banning demons from the bodies of those who came to him. That this was a gift shared by others is implied by Mark's story in which the disciples tell Jesus, "Teacher, we saw someone casting out demons in your name, and we tried to stop him, because he was not following us." But Jesus said, "Do not stop him; for no one who does a deed of power in my name will be able soon afterward to speak evil of me" (Mark 9:38–39). Jesus may have taught the gift to some Apostles, for later on, some of them were credited with healings as well.

There is another explanation for Jesus' ability to heal, of course; from a Christian perspective, Jesus had supernatural powers because he was the Son of God, and therefore he was able to do miraculous things.

In sum, there were plenty sources of evil and demons in Jesus' lifetime. For most, however, the most offensive form of evil was the Romans. It was the Romans and their vassal rulers, including Herod and his sons Archelaus and Antipas, who had introduced Roman customs, Roman paganism, and Roman luxuries onto the sacred soil of ancient Israel. And the focal point of all this hatred toward the Romans was a man who would ultimately determine Jesus' fate: a Roman named Pontius Pilatus, prefect of Judea. The Pontii were a minor family of Roman *equites*, or knights, whose burning ambition, shared by almost all other knightly clans, was to join the true aristocracy of Rome: the senatorial class. For a knight to gain the rank of senator, however, he not only had to have successfully completed a distinguished military and political career; he also had to show assets in excess of a million sesterces. The catch was that this fortune could not be accumulated through commerce, trade, or any form of financial speculation. That is why most senators owed their wealth to large agricultural estates, and why the Roman Senate was traditionally composed almost exclusively of landed peerage. For a knight whose family did not have impressive land holdings, or who did not have the fortune of having married a wealthy widow, there remained only one other avenue for advancement: the diplomatic service. Serving in the office of prefect or governor in one of the empire's far-flung possessions, one could do very well for oneself—by leveraging one's right, as Roman governor, to sell lucrative franchises, or to engage in all sorts of bribery and extortion, as Cicero's case against Gaius Verres may attest.

Roman governors were expected to govern with some wisdom and a sense of moderation, but Pilate revealed his contempt for the Jewish people right from the beginning. The first incident occurred soon after Pilate was appointed as the fifth prefect of

*A foundation stone from Caesarea with
the name "Pilate, Prefect of Judea"*

Judea in 26 CE. The reason may have been that, as everyone on the Palatine Hill knew, Judea was a bad posting. It had a restless population, it had no mines, no forests, no manufacturing, nor other major assets to speak of—nothing to sell or extort. But Pilate did have a certain freedom of movement. His immediate boss, Lucius Aelius Lamia, governor of Greater Syria, was not in Antioch but far away in the Roman capital.[9] This may have emboldened the prefect to take certain steps that would not have been tolerated if his superior had resided in Antioch, a mere five days' ride away.

And so, shortly after his arrival in Judea, Pilate decided on a deliberate provocation to test the Jewish mettle. He sent a cohort of Roman soldiers into the Antonia Fortress facing the Temple of Jerusalem and specifically ordered that the soldiers carry their ensigns in full view. These, as Roman custom demanded, prominently displayed the image of the emperor. As the citizens of Jerusalem woke up and entered the Temple precinct, they were shocked to find these idolatrous standards posted right opposite the Temple. An outcry ensued. When it transpired that the new prefect was ensconced in his residence in Caesarea, the people marched in protest to the seaside town. Pilate faced the protestors and declared that unless the crowd left Caesarea at once, he would order his soldiers to move in and kill everyone in sight. At this, the protesters threw themselves on the ground and bared their necks, ready to take the blade. They would rather accept death, their spokesman said, than to see their ancient laws trampled.

Pilate realized he was outfoxed. It would not do to begin his term with a bloodbath of such proportions. He ordered that the ensigns be removed from the Temple. But he never forgave the Jews their victory. From that day forward, he plotted his revenge. It was not long in coming. As we saw in Chapter 3, in 28 CE he conspired with the high priest Caiaphas to use the funds of the Temple treasury, the *korban*, to build an aqueduct to the city, which would have given him access to the one source of capital available in Judea. When word of this secret deal leaked, the nation rose in uproar. This time, Pilate had no compunction about unleashing his soldiers. The men and women who staged a protest in the forecourt of the Temple were slaughtered. Since the protestors were unarmed and their attackers were professional soldiers, says Josephus, "a great many were killed; many others were wounded."[10]

Until this time, Rome had represented the rule of law; a harsh law, certainly, but not a rule without a certain sense of justice. The Roman *Ius Gentium,* the codex of law pertaining to non-Roman citizens in occupied territories, explicitly granted subject peoples the law of petition: the right to make their grievances known to their governing body, provided this was done in an orderly and nonviolent fashion.[11] With his bloody strike, Pilate had dispelled the fiction that Rome's occupation of Judea was essentially a benevolent one. What's more, his actions signaled to Rome's other vassal rulers in the region—including Antipas—that Rome fully sanctioned the use of preemptive terror to maintain public order. For many Judeans, Pilate now became the personification of evil. And as the Gospels tell us, it is that evil that Jesus himself would taste at the end of his ministry.

But what does the verse *and deliver us from evil* mean for us today? Are there still sources of evil in our world? Have we advanced in any significant way from the days of Jesus? The answer, without question, is that there is still evil, intolerance, and violence in the world, albeit in different forms. We only have to watch the nightly news or follow social media to see that in autocracies around the world, the rights of men and particularly women are suppressed on a daily basis. But what about democracies like the United States?

On the one hand, there is ample evidence that human beings, at home and abroad, have advanced in the last two centuries or so. As I wrote in my book *The Ultimate Visual History of the World,* despite the hardship of working in nineteenth-century factories the Industrial Revolution caused the standard of living to rise, after its long decline in the eighteenth century. The cost of food dropped thanks to improvements in production and transportation, thus improving the diet and health of the general population. Literacy rates also rose in the Victorian

Era, and 86 percent of the world population can now read and write. Because of the efforts of the United Nations and countless charitable institutions, 200,000 new people gain access to fresh, piped water every day. In the twentieth century, NATO and the Warsaw Pact deployed more than 140,000 nuclear weapons. Today, that number is down to 60,000.

But in other areas, the United States is a nation that appears to be regressing in terms of its ability to preserve and protect its citizens, in all states, and across all demographics. In 2021, the violent crime rate was still 395 cases per 100,000 Americans.[12] While it is true that overall crime is lower than during its peak in the late 1980s and early 1990s, violent crime causes havoc in our communities, costing an estimated $4.9 trillion in 2021 alone. This includes domestic violence against women as well as robberies, theft, and aggravated assault.

But the great scourge of our time is violence out of the barrel of a gun. The statistics are devastating: in 2022 alone, there were 619 mass shootings that killed 296 children. Imagine, for a moment, the lives that these nearly 300 children would have lived before they were senselessly murdered on the cusp of life. I am blessed with five grandchildren, and I asked them whether there had been any mass-shooting drills at their school. Some of them, including my youngest granddaughter who is five years old, were traumatized by these drills—to say nothing about their parents who live in fear every time they drop their kids off at school. Why do we tolerate this threat to our children? Why do we accept the widespread availability of weapons of mass destruction, such as the AR-15 assault machine gun?

While the Second Amendment gives American citizens the right to bear arms, strictly for self-defense, the type of gun the authors of this amendment had in mind was the single-shot musket.

They did not specify weapons of mass destruction, which in 1791 was the cannon. As Esau McCaulley wrote in a *New York Times* Opinion piece, gun advocates in America are prone to blame mass shootings on "evil" in society, but they refuse any legislation to ban such military-style machine guns. "It does not matter that America far outpaces other nations in mass shootings," he wrote; "we must have an unexplainable abundance of evil hearts here," in the United States.[13] But if we continue that line of reasoning, it means that American society is by definition more evil than other First World nations, who have far lower rates of gun violence because of their rigorous laws limiting gun ownership.

Perhaps the source of that evil is that for many people, the gun replaces reasoning. It is far easier to walk around and intimidate people with a gun in your hand than to try to persuade them of the righteousness of your ideas.

Governments cannot control or restrain the evil in our hearts, but they can restrain the ability of evil hearts to do violence to those around them. In that sense, slavery was a horrific evil in America until the Federal Government moved to abolish it in 1863. Similarly, the evil of mass killings will continue to proliferate in our nation until we move to abolish it, by keeping weapons like AR-type assault rifles off our streets. For Christians who cherish life, both born and unborn, this should be a matter of the highest priority.

| 11 |

RECONSTRUCTING THE PASSION

In the preceding chapters, we have traced the origins and development of Jesus' ministry in its historical context, and explored the essential focus of his movement: an effort to redefine the Judaism of his time as a society based on the three pillars of the Torah: faith in God, social justice, and human compassion. We then examined the Lord's Prayer in the context of that focus, and discovered the meaning behind each of its beautiful verses that can serve as an inspiration for us to be pro-active in our communities—and to serve as a beacon of hope and love.

We cannot conclude this argument, however, without examining with that same historical lens the events that for many Christians serve as the essential purpose of Jesus' life: his crucifixion on the cross so as to expiate our sins and redeem all of humankind. We can safely assume that the crucifixion of

Jesus was a historical event; even Josephus wrote that "there was about this time Jesus, a wise man . . . for he was a doer of wonderful works. . . . And when Pilate . . . had condemned him to the cross, those that loved him at the first did not cease to be attached to him."[1]

In what would become his most cohesive theological argument, his Letter to the Romans, Paul wrote that "God proves his love for us in that while we still were sinners Christ died for us. Much more surely then, now that we have been justified by his blood, will we be saved through him from the wrath of God" (Romans 5:8–9). In other words, for mainstream Christianity the Passion is *the* quintessential moment in Jesus' ministry. And here we must grapple with two different perspectives: the traditional view, which argues that Jesus' death on the cross was pre-ordained from the very beginning by God (John 3:16–17); and the historical view, which suggests that nothing that Jesus did during his ministry could in any way be conceived as a crime warranting a death sentence. Instead, that historical analysis suggests that Jesus' death on the cross was the result of an exceptional converge of motives and events.

To understand this dilemma, we should first return to Paul's efforts to spread the word of Jesus among the mostly Gentile population of Asia Minor—a group that Paul himself refers to as "the Greek" (Romans 2:9). Interestingly, Paul (then named Saul) began his career as a leader of those who energetically persecuted the Jesus movement in the weeks and months after the Easter events. Saul was aware that these followers had spread across Judea and suspected that they were trying to lie low in places beyond the reach of Jerusalem. "Still breathing threats and murder against the disciples," he went to the high priest and asked for authorization to extend his net beyond Judea, even as far as Damascus in Syria. He was determined to find "any who belonged to the Way, men or women," and bring them bound to Jerusalem (Acts 9:2). But on the way to Damascus, Saul experienced a conversion (Acts 9:18). He was baptized, and "immediately began to proclaim Jesus in the synagogues."

A native of Tarsus, the capital of Cilicia, Paul had been born into a Jewish family but held honorary Roman citizenship as a result of that city's faithful remittance of the annual tribute to Rome. As we saw, Tarsus was renowned as a center of philosophical discourse. Philosophers flocked to Tarsus in the hope of finding patronage. As a result, Paul's sharp intellect drank in the Greek oratory of the street. Even after Paul was educated in Jerusalem by Pharisees, including the distinguished Rabbi Gamaliel, he remained fond of the philosophical dialectic that was the bread and butter of his home town.

It was a world far removed from the illiterate peasant culture of Jesus' Lower Galilee. Paul understood this and, with the supreme confidence of an educated Pharisee, saw that he alone had the intellect to turn Jesus' following into a proper religious movement. He must have grasped that without the charismatic presence of Jesus himself, his Jewish movement would eventually fizzle and go the way of other would-be reformers—notably, John the Baptist. And in that sense he was correct; the original Jesus movement, now led by Jesus' brother James, slowly succumbed to intense persecution. According to the fourth-century Bishop Eusebius of Caesarea, they ultimately fled to Pella, in the Decapolis, where it may have died out.

The problem was, as Paul discovered during his journeys through the Greek world of Asia Minor (now Turkey), that the Jewish communities of this region rejected his claim that Jesus was the long-awaited Messiah, who as countless prophets had foretold

The ancient city of Pella, in today's Kingdom of Jordan, where the remnants of the Jewish Jesus movement may have fled after the First Jewish War.

would liberate the people of Israel. How could they accept Jesus as the Messiah though he had *not* cleansed the land of pagan occupation, and instead, had been crucified as a common criminal?

In contrast, Paul found that many Greeks were intrigued by his teachings and were attracted to the simplicity and nobility of a religion that recognized but one God. A God, moreover, who was merciful and just, unlike the hedonistic gods of Rome who were more concerned with pleasure than with the well-being of humankind. But he also recognized that the more onerous precepts of Judaism—circumcision, the dietary laws, the strict limitations of the Sabbath—were a deterrent for many of these "God-fearing" people. As we saw, he therefore uncoupled the Jesus movement from its roots in Second Temple Judaism and its search for a more compassionate, just, and faithful society. Instead, he argued that God is the creator of us all, Jew and Greek alike, and that through his sacrifice on the cross, Jesus had replaced the validity of the Jewish Law, the Torah. "We hold that a person is justified by faith apart from the works prescribed by the law," Paul wrote (Romans 3:28). In the process, Jesus "Christ" effectively replaced the Law as the principal conduit between humankind and God, and as the principal agency of salvation.

Paul's emphatic use of the term "Jesus Christ" played a key role in this argument. In a strictly Jewish context, *Christos* meant "Anointed One," the title of the "Messiah" (*Msheekha* in Aramaic, *Mashiach* in Hebrew) who would lead the people of Israel. By definition, the Messiah was a descendant of King David and therefore a "son of God"—that is, a man favored by God and anointed by his divine Spirit (2 Samuel 7:14). Knowing that the meaning of the word "Messiah" would be utterly lost on his Greek audience, Paul translated the term "Jesus Christ" to mean that he was not *a* son of the Jewish God, but *the* Son of the universal God, of the same divine substance as the Father. It is this idea that upset his Jewish audience more than anything else. They could accept the idea of the immortality of the soul—after all, the Pharisees had said the same thing—but the idea that a Jew could consider himself just as divine as Yahweh himself violated everything that ancient Judaism stood for.

Paul's Gentile audience saw that differently. They had been raised in a Roman culture where gods could comingle with mortal women at will and create demigods like Hercules. For them, being the Son of God had to have a *physical* rather than a purely spiritual manifestation; the idea that a human could become a divine being was readily accepted, unlike in Jewish circles. Thus, Paul preached that Jesus was the Son of God by virtue of his resurrection, and that "death no longer had any dominion over him" (Romans 6:9). And that, Paul said, was the essence of God's great gift to humankind, for all those who had faith would likewise be resurrected and have "an eternal life in Christ Jesus our Lord" (Romans 6:23). This core belief became the key to the tremendous success that Christianity would garner in the Greco-Roman world. These Gentiles felt a deep attraction to the joyous teachings of a man who said that the righteous would find salvation in heaven, regardless of their station in life.

This idea has since become a foundation of Christianity, and indeed one of the few articles of faith that all branches of Christianity agree on. It could therefore be argued that the Christian movement that has persisted over the centuries and is still alive today is, from a strictly theological point of view, the work of the mind of Paul, rather than that of Jesus. Paul justified his ideas by saying that he felt guided by Jesus' spirit; as he wrote, "We have the mind of Christ" (1 Corinthians 2:16).

At the same time, however, a purely historical analysis of the Passion story will arrive at a different conclusion; not that Jesus was crucified (which is a matter of historical record, both in the Gospels and the writings of Josephus), but whether this crucifixion was truly the product of predestination from the very beginning. The Gospels, which were written under the influence of Pauline theology, insert passages that suggest that Jesus was aware of what was awaiting him in Jerusalem. "He then began to teach them that the Son of Man must suffer many things and be rejected by the elders, the chief priests and the teachers of the law," Mark writes, "and that he must be killed and after three days rise again" (Mark 8:31).

In fact, Mark's Gospel develops the argument that as Jesus' ministry unfolded, it prompted a growing opposition from the elites of the land, and that Jesus' arrest and execution was the result of a carefully laid conspiracy. The core of this opposition, Mark claims, were the Sadducees and the Pharisees, as well as the scribes. After Jesus heals a man with a withered hand, Mark says, "the Pharisees went out and immediately conspired with the Herodians against him, how to destroy him" (Mark 3:6). Later in the story, when Jesus is teaching in the Temple, the chief priests "sent him some Pharisees and Herodians to trap him in what he said" (Mark 12:13).

With all due respect to Mark, this presumed conspiracy is unlikely because as we saw, the Sadducees, the Pharisees, and the Herodian dynasty were deeply opposed to one another. To argue that these mutual enemies were somehow in collusion to destroy a rural rabbi from Galilee is historically difficult to defend. The reason why Mark came up with the conspiracy theory, I believe, is that Mark wrote his Gospel in Rome for Roman Christians, and that it would have been very difficult for him to make the Romans, and specifically their prefect Pontius Pilate, the villains of the story, even though they clearly were. Clinical psychologists refer to this process as "displacement theory." As a result, Mark shifted the blame for Jesus' death from the Romans to all the principal Jewish groups that, as he learned from oral traditions, were active in Jesus' time and made them by association responsible for Jesus' death. And yet, as we will see, Mark's Gospel is extremely important for other reasons, not in the least because it is the oldest extant report about the Passion and, therefore, closest to the historical events.

I realize that this is a difficult subject for many devout Christians, and if you feel uncomfortable with this line of reasoning, I suggest that you skip the remainder of this chapter and move to the next one.

Jerusalem at the time of Jesus

Map of Jerusalem in Jesus' time, including the location of the Upper Room or Last Supper room; Gethsemane; Herod's Palace; the Antonia Fortress; and the Temple.

We have seen how, at one point, it was the Pharisees who warned Jesus that Herod Antipas, tetrarch of Galilee, was searching for him with the intent to arrest and kill him, just as he had done with John the Baptist. "At that time some Pharisees came to Jesus and said to him, 'Leave this place and go somewhere else,'" Luke writes. "Herod wants to kill you" (Luke 13:31). This passage does not appear in the other Gospels, except for an oblique reference in Mark, where Jesus warns his followers: "Be careful . . . Watch out for the yeast of the Pharisees and that of Herod" (Mark 8:15). There is, however, little question that if Jesus indeed attracted the large crowds described in the Gospels, this would eventually have been reported to Herod Antipas. As Josephus wrote, Antipas was obsessed with the threat of dissident movements that could conceivably have the power to topple him, which was the reason (at least in Josephus' view) why the tetrarch moved against John the Baptist and eventually had him killed.

Judea was a different situation, however. Even though Pilate was an intensely cruel and vindictive man who had no compunction about ordering a wholesale massacre of peaceful protestors, as he had done in 28 CE, it is doubtful that he would have been aware of Jesus' movements. Up to this point, these had been limited to Galilee and the territory to the north, including Phoenicia and the Decapolis. Pilate's remit ended at the borders of Judea, and troublesome *hasidim* or "holy men" in Galilee and Perea were not his problem, but that of Antipas. What's more—and this point is often overlooked in descriptions of the Passion story—Pilate had inherited a system whereby a line was drawn between purely domestic and religious cases, which fell under the jurisdiction of the Great Sanhedrin, the Jewish Council, and political cases, including any form of political agitation against the sovereignty of Rome, which were the responsibility of the Roman prefect. Therefore, anyone accused of blasphemy or any other religious offense was indicted and tried by the Sanhedrin, and if necessary punished with a flogging or a death sentence. For example, the Mishnah tractate *Sanhedrin* describes the terms by which a "false prophet" may, or may not, be put on trial and put to death (Mishnah Sanhedrin 11:5). The Romans didn't figure in this equation; they had other things to worry about.

What we do know is that Jesus' decision to move his ministry from Galilee to Jerusalem on or about Passover of 30 CE (the exact year continues to be debated) was a logical one. His ministry in Galilee had run its course, and much to his disappointment, it had not borne the fruits he had hoped for. The tax collectors and landowners were still extorting the peasants. The homeless hadn't found any shelter. The chronically ill were still ostracized from their villages. "Woe to you, Chorazin!" Jesus cries in the Gospels of Luke and Matthew; "Woe to you, Bethsaida! If the powerful deeds performed among you had been done in Tyre and Sidon, they would have changed their ways long ago, sitting in sackcloth and ashes!" (Matthew 11:21; Luke 10:13).

This is the moment when Jesus decided on a new and very different strategy: to take his movement to the heartland of Judea. To some extent, I believe the decision may have been informed by the example of the great prophets of the Hebrew Bible, particularly Jeremiah. Like the prophet Amos, Jeremiah was deeply engaged with the growing rift between rich and poor in Judah's society. And like Jesus, Jeremiah taught that only a return to the precepts of the Torah, rather than the sacrificial cult, would save Israel (Jeremiah 22:3–8). These teachings culminated in a famous sermon that the prophet delivered at the Temple. According to Jeremiah, God told him to "stand in the gate of the Lord's house and say, 'Hear the word of the Lord, all you people of Judah'" (Jeremiah 7:2). In fact, once in Jerusalem Jesus would actually quote from Jeremiah's sermon, standing in the same place, the forecourt of the Second Temple, some 500 years later.

Thus Jesus and his followers set out on the long journey to Jerusalem. Just two miles before reaching the walls of Jerusalem, they entered the village of Bethany, located on the eastern slopes of the Mount of Olives. Here lived two relatives, Mary and Martha, to whom Jesus appears to have been close. It was a convenient place for Jesus and his immediate followers to eat, to rest, and mentally prepare themselves for the final ascent to the Temple.

The next morning, they must have been amazed to see the great Temple rise above the city, its golden cornices reflecting the light of the sun. The Roman author Pliny, an experienced globetrotter, called Jerusalem "by far the most famous city, not only of Judea, but of the whole East." Even today, watching the sun rise behind the Mount of Olives in the early morning to bathe the walls of the city with saffron-tinted light is a breathtaking experience. From Bethany, Jesus and his followers would have descended into the Valley of Kidron and from there slowly made their way toward the Temple complex, using a set of stairs to the Double Gate that were only excavated after the Six Day War in 1967.

They were not alone. For days now, thousands of Jews from all over Judea, Galilee, and the Diaspora had made their way to Jerusalem to offer their Passover sacrifice. The Passover festival, or *Pesach* in Hebrew, commemorates Israel's release from bondage in Egypt after an angel of God killed all of Egypt's

The (now restored) stairs to the Double Gate of the Temple, excavated in the late 1960s.

firstborn sons. To mark their homes as Israelite, rather than Egyptian, the Israelites had been told to sacrifice a lamb and paint the door lintel with its blood. All such homes were spared, or "passed over," by the angel's wrath (Exodus 12:6–7). Then, while waiting for the signal to leave Egypt, the Israelites were told to roast a lamb and eat it with unleavened bread, since there was no time to allow the bread to rise. The Torah instructed them to observe this event every year, in perpetuity (Exodus 12:25).

As soon as the great doors of the sanctuary swung open, the first mass of pilgrims surged into the vast open forecourt, known as the Court of the Gentiles. They then climbed the fifteen unevenly raised stairs to the gates—uneven, so that one had to ascend with care and reverence—and passed into the Court of Women. This was as far as Jewish women were allowed to go.

They were expected to remain there, in prayer, while their husbands continued on to the next court, their bleating lambs in tow, destined for the slaughter.

But Jesus never got this far. As we saw, Jesus' great Temple sermon was pre-empted by the high priest's decision to move the sale of pascal lambs and the requisite exchange of currency into the forecourt proper. As soon as they entered the Temple area, Jesus and the Apostles were jostled on all sides by pilgrims desperate to get to the front of the waiting queues for the moneychangers and the pens holding the lambs. The air would have been filled with the bleating of sheep, the cries of the pilgrims, and the voices of the moneychangers loudly proclaiming their exchange rates. Above it rose the stink of rotting fruit, animal dung, and sweating bodies in the sun, permeated by the odor of burnt flesh wafting from the Temple altar.

Jesus was shocked; this was not the setting he had imagined. He then rose in anger and, as we saw, "began to drive out those who were selling and those who were buying in the temple, and he overturned the tables of the money changers" (Mark 11:15).

Of course, this action did not go unnoticed. For days now, the Temple Guards and the Roman cohort stationed at the Antonia Fortress overlooking the Temple had been on high alert to suppress exactly this type of protest. The Temple Massacre of 28 CE was still fresh on everyone's mind. And then Jesus compounded his provocative action by loudly declaring, "Is it not written, 'My house shall be called a house of prayer for all the nations?' But you have made it a den of thieves" (Mark 11:17).

A den of thieves. As soon as these words were reported to the high priest Caiaphas, he must have been outraged. It was only a few years ago that Caiaphas and Pilate had colluded in pilfering the Temple treasury in order to finance a new aqueduct, to be built under Pilate's supervision. And here was this Galilean rabbi, who had not only disrupted the holiest day on the Temple calendar, but also tried to revive the accusation that the high priest was nothing but a thief. Jesus was actually quoting from Jeremiah's Temple Sermon, "Has this house, which is called by my name, become a den of robbers?" (Jeremiah 7:11), but that must have escaped the chief priests; the Sadducees did not believe that the Books of the Prophets were divinely inspired Scripture. Mark tells us that as soon as "the chief priests and the scribes heard it, they kept looking for a way to kill him" (Mark 11:18). And for good reason. Who knew what kind of support this Galilean rabbi had in the city? Did the action against the moneychangers serve as a signal for a wholesale uprising against the chief priests and the Romans?

And so, the warrant went out for Jesus' arrest—not because of a carefully laid conspiracy that had been brewing for many months, but because of Jesus' sudden and unprovoked attack on the merchants who were lawfully selling their sacrificial animals in the Temple forecourt. But the Temple Guards didn't move fast enough. Before they could reach Jesus, he and his followers had slipped out of the Temple. Nonetheless, Jesus was now a marked man.

Many historians agree that it was Jesus' attack on the moneychangers that led to the call for his arrest. Neither the Romans nor the chief priests could ignore the risk that this Galilean rabbi might try to stage another violent demonstration, if not in the Temple, then elsewhere in Jerusalem's crowded streets. That is why Jesus decided to hide in plain sight, in a city overflowing with pilgrims, rather than returning to Bethany. He knew that the city gates and the roads would be heavily guarded.

As we saw previously, Jesus and his disciples then found a place to have their *Seder* together. After darkness had fallen, they left the city amidst the throngs of worshippers returning to the Mount of Olives, where thousands of families were camping out in the open. That is where Jesus was identified by Judas—possibly the only man who could have picked him out among the multitudes crowding the hill—and where he was arrested. What is so remarkable about this dramatic moment is that Jesus was surprisingly calm during his arrest. In fact, his only concern was for the men and women who had accompanied him. In John's Gospel, the Temple Guards ask Jesus if he is the one they're looking for. "I am he," is the response; "so, if you seek me, let these men go" (John 18:8). According to Mark, the disciples didn't think twice and promptly fled into the night (Mark 14:50).

Jesus' calm demeanor, so in contrast to the report of his agony in the garden (Mark 14:33–36), is perhaps not surprising when we imagine that the prospect of facing the Sanhedrin, of having his day in court, would not have fazed him in the least. In fact, he may have welcomed it; it's why he came to Jerusalem. Jesus was a skilled debater, and he may have been confident that, at the very least, he could persuade the Pharisee faction on the council of the righteousness of his cause. And that's no mere speculation. In the Book of Acts, it is a Pharisee, the highly respected Rabbi Gamaliel, grandson of the great Rabbi Hillel, who launched into a defense of the Apostles in front of the Sanhedrin. He argued that if their works "are not of human origin, but of God's, you will not be able to overthrow them!" (Acts 5:38–42). And indeed, the Apostles were later released. No prophet in the Hebrew Bible had ever been condemned to death for preaching the coming of the Kingdom of God, or for criticizing the yawning gap between the elites (including the priesthood) and the vast masses of the poor. True, Jesus had upstaged the stalls of the moneychangers, and no doubt a thorough beating was in store, but it would be worth it if this would allow him to address the highest religious authority in the land. After all, the same had happened to Jeremiah, who after his incendiary speech in the Temple was arrested by Pashhur, chief officer of the Temple Guard, and after a beating was thrown in the Temple stockade. But the next day, he was released (Jeremiah 20:1–3).

The same thing came to pass when the Apostles were arrested in the weeks and months after the crucifixion and resurrection. They were held in Temple custody overnight and subsequently arraigned during a full session presided by "Annas the [former] high priest, [and] Caiaphas" (Acts 4:3; 5:17). After a passionate defense delivered by Peter, they were released.

From a strictly historical perspective, therefore, there was no reason to think that a death sentence lay in store for Jesus, and certainly not by the Romans, who had neither the jurisdiction nor the inclination to intervene in what, on the surface at least, was a case of blasphemy.

Everything that happens from this point on is based on one source, the Gospel of Mark; the other evangelists merely follow his example, while adding various interpolations and dialogue. Some scholars, including John Dominic Crossan, believe that the Passion in Mark is based on an older document, now lost, known as the "Cross Gospel." Fragments of this Cross Gospel may have survived in another Christian text, the so-called Gospel of Peter, which was discovered in Egypt in 1886. Though church fathers from the third to the sixth century did not deem this document sufficiently authoritative for inclusion in the canon of the New Testament, there is some indication that the Gospel of Peter enjoyed wide popularity in the centuries to come. Unlike "sayings documents" like Thomas and Q, the Gospel of Peter provides a concise narrative of the Passion events, with details that somewhat deviate from the version described in the New Testament.[2]

According to Mark, then, Jesus was taken to the house of the high priest, where the chief priests were assembled. This was entirely without precedent. As we just saw, the established procedure specified that the accused should be held in the Temple stockade until such time that a full quorum of the Sanhedrin could hear his case. Since this was Passover, followed by the Sabbath, no such hearing would have been in the offing for several days. But the high priest actually used this to his advantage. Caiaphas must have known that in the highly partisan atmosphere of the Sanhedrin, the Pharisaic members might very well object to Jesus being indicted, let alone sentenced to death. As we just saw, the subsequent events bear this out; whenever the Apostles were dragged in front of the Jewish Council, they were invariably released after the Pharisees came to their defense. That is why Caiaphas used the hiatus of the Passover festival to spirit Jesus to his home, where he could conduct an indictment, in secret, in front of a hand-picked group of Sadducee priests, exactly as Mark's Gospel tells us. The personal insult of *a den of thieves* was simply too much to bear; he had to nip this protest in the bud before it could spread across the city.

A priestly mansion, excavated in the late 1960s by Israeli archaeologist Nahman Avigad, helps us to set the stage. A dwelling on multiple levels: a private *mikveh* on the lower floor, stairs to the main level, and there, surrounded by painted stucco panels, a large meeting room with mosaic floors, measuring

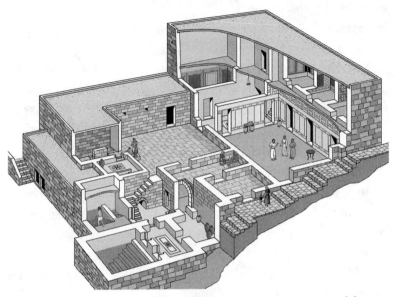

Reconstruction of the Priestly Mansion by Leen Ritmeyer, excavated from 1969 onward.

thirty-three by twenty-one square feet. It faces a large open courtyard, accessible from the street. The Gospel of Mark says that it was in exactly such a courtyard that Peter stood warming his hands by the fire, while Jesus was arraigned inside. During the month of Nisan, or early April, nights in Jerusalem could still be quite cold. One of the high priest's servant girls spotted Peter there and said, "You also were with Jesus, the man from Nazareth." Peter, afraid that he might be arrested as well, denied it. "I do not know or understand what you are talking about," he said, and left (Mark 14:66–72).

Inside, the indictment had begun as soon as Jesus was brought into the meeting room. This was a violation of the prevailing law, because according to the Mishnah "a tribe, a false prophet, or a high priest can only be tried by a court of seventy-one judges" (Mishnah Sanhedrin 1:5). But Caiaphas didn't care; he wanted to get the proceedings over with as quickly as possible. An example had to be set: blasphemy against the Temple and an invective against the priesthood would not be tolerated.

And so the chief priests conferred. What could they accuse him of? After all, the legalities had to be observed. Fortunately, some "witnesses" had come forward, no doubt in expectation of a reward. "We heard him say," said some, "I will destroy this temple that is made with hands, and in three days I will build another, not made with hands" (Mark 14:57–58). An unwelcome prophecy, to be sure, but not a capital crime; many prophets had foretold the very same thing. Growing exasperated, the high priest asked Jesus, "Have you no answer? What is it that they testify against you?" (Mark 14:60). But Jesus remained silent. He now realized that he was not going to be heard by the full Sanhedrin, and that the outcome of this sham indictment was a foregone conclusion. If that were the case, he was not going to dignify the proceedings by giving a response.

But Caiaphas was a crafty man. He eyed Jesus and asked slyly, "Are you the Messiah, the Son of the Blessed One?" That was a question that Jesus could not ignore. It went to the heart of what his ministry was all about. Jesus responded by quoting the "Son of Man" verse from the Book of Daniel with which he so closely identified himself. Throughout his ministry, he had always referred to himself as the "Son of Man," *ben adam*; in the four canonical Gospels the term appears no fewer than eighty-one times. "You will see the Son of Man seated at the right hand of the Power," he said, "and coming with the clouds of heaven," quoting from Daniel 7:13–14 and Psalm 110:1 (Mark 14:62). Hearing this, the high priest got up and tore his clothes, the biblical way of expressing righteous anger. But inwardly,

Caiaphas was exultant. "Why do we still need witnesses?" he cried in Mark's Gospel. "You have heard his blasphemy! What is your decision?" And, says Mark, "All of them condemned him as deserving death" (Mark 14:63–64).

The reason for Caiaphas' glee is not difficult to understand. Outwardly, there is nothing in Jesus' words that would have qualified for capital punishment. He had merely quoted from the Book of Daniel and the Psalms, even though the Sadducees did not recognize these books as Scripture. But Caiaphas had known all along that he faced a problem. Yes, he could secure a death sentence from his small group of cronies, but he was powerless to carry it out. Only a full quorum of all seventy-one members of the Great Sanhedrin had the authority to put a man to death. For example, the Temple precinct beyond the forecourt was marked by a low fence called the *soreg*. Marble tablets were posted at intervals of a hundred paces, warning any Gentile trespasser that if he was found beyond this boundary, he would be stoned to death. This explicitly granted the Sanhedrin the authority to condemn those who violated the sanctity of the Temple. Paul discovered this to his discomfort when he was accused of taking Gentiles past the *soreg* and only escaped execution by appealing to his right, as a Roman citizen, to a proper trial under Roman law.

But Caiaphas didn't have a quorum of the Sanhedrin. Even if he had assembled all seventy-one members, which was unlikely, they wouldn't have fit in his house.[3] Ergo, he did not have the means to have Jesus executed. The only authority who did have this power were the Romans. But as we saw, the Romans did not get involved in matters involving the Temple, or accusations of blasphemy. That was the hard-won prerequisite of the Sanhedrin. The challenge for Caiaphas, therefore, was to

*The soreg stone, warning Gentile trespassers
of the penalty of death.*

spin the case against Jesus from the religious into the political
sphere. If he could somehow argue that the defendant, based
on his own testimony, was not a threat to the Temple but to
the political order of Roman Judea, he would be compelled, as
a law-abiding high priest, to transfer the case to Roman jurisdiction. And Jesus had just given him that sort of testimony! A
man "seated at the right hand of the power, coming with the
clouds of heaven"? That sounded very much like a man plotting

the political overthrow of the Roman occupation. And given his past dealings with Pilate, who happened to be in town to supervise the security arrangements during Passover, Caiaphas was confident that the prefect would promptly act on this extradition and pronounce a death sentence against Jesus. It would serve as a perfect object lesson for the thousands of Jews now crowding the streets of Jerusalem.

And so it came to pass, exactly as Caiaphas had hoped. Jesus was transferred to Roman custody. A brief hearing was held, presided by Pontius Pilate. The charge was read—the prisoner is accused of claiming to be the Messiah, "the King of the Jews"—and Jesus' response, "You say so," was noted for the record (Mark 15:2). Pilate then asked if Jesus wanted to say something in his defense, but Jesus remained quiet. He understood that this hearing was a mere formality. His fate was already sealed.

| *An ossuary, believed to have contained the bones of the high priest Caiaphas.*

He would be condemned to die by crucifixion—the inevitable punishment for anyone caught in a rebellious act—without ever having had the opportunity to speak to the multitudes in Jerusalem, the very reason why he had come to the city.

Nor did he have any opportunity to have character witnesses speak on his behalf, as would be the case if this were a Roman trial. But the sad fact is that Jesus did not merit a proper trial; not under the *Ius Civile*, notwithstanding the lengthy proceedings described in the Gospel of John. Unlike Paul, Jesus was a colonial subject, and colonials were judged by the *Ius Gentium*, the "law for foreign nationals," which gave the local magistrate wide latitude in judging offenders as he saw fit.

That is why the brief hearing described by Mark is probably closer to the truth than the more elaborate trial developed by Luke, Matthew, and John, who may have witnessed actual Roman trials in their own towns. In their versions, Pilate is depicted as a compassionate man who is genuinely vexed by Jesus' innocence. "I cannot find a case against this man," Pilate proclaims in front of a large crowd of Jews, who inexplicably had gained access to this hearing (John 18:38). The purpose of this device is to shift the blame for Jesus' murder from the Roman prefect to the Jews. As John writes, "From then on Pilate tried to release him, but the Jews cried out, 'If you release this man, you are no friend of Caesar'" (John 19:12). And thus Pilate washed his hands of the whole affair and had Jesus taken away to be crucified.

Mark introduces another exculpatory motif: an amnesty proceeding, whereby Pilate offered the crowd attending the hearing a choice: should he release Jesus or a notorious criminal called Barrabas? As Mark portrays the scene, the chief priests immediately went to work. "They stirred up the crowd to have him

The Kishle building, where Israeli archaeologists discovered remains of Herod's Palace, the presumed location of the hearing by Pilate.

release Barabbas for them instead. Pilate spoke to them again, 'Then what do you wish me to do with the man you call the King of the Jews?' They shouted back, 'Crucify him!'" (Mark 15:13).

And thus, the blame for Jesus' death was neatly shifted from the Romans, in whose empire the evangelists and countless missionaries like Paul hoped to find fertile ground for Christianity, to the bloodthirsty Jews attending the "trial." But the truth is different. Pilate, as we have seen, was a man who from the beginning of his term deliberately provoked Jewish sensitivities and wasted no time in crushing anyone whom he deemed a political liability. "Pilate," says the Jewish historian Philo, writing around 41 CE, "[used] briberies, insults, robberies, outrages, wanton injuries, [and] constantly repeated executions without trial." A man, in short, of "ceaseless and supremely grievous cruelty."[4]

Not a man who would have shed a tear by condemning an innocent man like Jesus on trumped-up charges.

Instead, the blame was placed on the Jews of Judea, who in 66 CE rose up in revolt against the Roman occupation, forcing Rome to dispatch a large expeditionary force. For Mark, who wrote his Gospel in the wake of this revolt, it was easy to make the "terrorists" of Roman Judea the culprit of the story. What's more, in the latter half of the first century large numbers of Jewish Christians were ostracized, banned from synagogues, and in some quarters even persecuted. Since the rabbinical hierarchy rejected Jesus as the Messiah, it stood to reason that they were the ones who had condemned Jesus to begin with. "His blood be on us, and on our children!" the priests cry in Matthew's account (Matthew 27:25).

We cannot fault the evangelists for conveying the tensions of Early Christianity. The rejection of Jesus by Jewish communities stung, for Jesus had been a Jewish rabbi himself. What the evangelists did not anticipate, however, is that by shifting the blame for Jesus' murder from the Romans to the *Sippenhaft*, the collective guilt of Judaism as a whole, they were laying the moral justification for centuries of anti-Semitic persecution to come.

EPILOGUE

THE SPLINTERING OF CHRISTIANITY

At the beginning of this book we saw how much American Christianity has diverged, not only in terms of its many denominations but also with regard to its polarizing political viewpoints. What this book has tried to show is that the only way to bridge these great divides is to return to the essential precepts that Jesus taught us. After all, if we don't try to follow in his path and adhere to his teachings, by what right can we call ourselves Christians?

The term "Christian" was first coined in Antioch, Syria, before Paul and Barnabas arrived in the city. Some scholars believe the term was used by the city's inhabitants in a pejorative sense, to mock the community of Jesus followers (Acts 11:26). But these disciples wore the name as a badge of honor, for they truly believed that they were living and acting the way Jesus had taught them.

In 66 CE, the First Jewish War broke out in Roman Palestine, which cast Jews and Jewish Christians alike in a bad light throughout the empire. It is perhaps no coincidence that the first attempt to collect the sayings of Jesus into a comprehensive, theological story—the Gospel of Mark—was undertaken in this period of tension and anxiety. Just as Rabbinic Judaism would seek comfort in the reassuring certainty of Scripture after the Jewish War, so too did Early Christianity.

Surprisingly, however, Emperor Vespasian—the man who had led the expeditionary forces to suppress the Jewish War—recognized the value of Jewish communities throughout the empire and never revoked the status of Judaism as an officially licensed religion. Unfortunately, the same could not be said for the Christian movement; that religion remained unlawful, though Vespasian was too busy restoring the empire's solvency

| *A first-century bust of Emperor Vespasian.*

after Emperor Nero's chaotic administration to concern himself with religious persecution. This changed with Vespasian's son Domitian, who according to Bishop Eusebius launched a severe persecution of Christians. Scholars are conflicted whether it is this persecution that inspired the writing of the Book of Revelation. While some believe that the reference to the "beast" in Revelation 13:16, as the number 666, refers to "Nero Caesar," other indications, including references to "Babylon" as code for Rome clearly places the work in the final decades of the first century.

From a strictly historical perspective, however, there is no evidence that at this point in time Christians were persecuted throughout the realm as the result of official Roman policy. Historians therefore believe that such persecutions were usually prompted by local tensions between Christians and their neighbors who continued to adhere to the official Roman cult. Emperor Trajan, who took power in 98 CE, had little interest in religious persecution and devoted his time instead to expanding the Roman Empire, capturing Armenia, the Nabatean Kingdom (with its capital of Petra) and much of the Parthian Empire up to the Persian Gulf. When one of Trajan's governors, the younger Pliny, boasted of his pursuit of suspected Christians in Bithynia, Trajan berated him and wondered if he had not something better to do.

Still, local persecutions persisted. The Christian author Tertullian, who was active in Carthage in Roman Africa (today's Tunis) during the second half of the second century, captured the prevailing mood against Christians by writing that "they think the Christians [are] the cause of every public disaster, of every affliction with which the people are visited. If the Tiber rises as high as the city walls, if the Nile does not send its waters up over the fields, if the heavens give no rain, if there is an earthquake, if there is famine or pestilence, straightway the cry is, 'Away with the Christians to the lion!'"[1]

And yet, the Christian movement continued to grow, buoyed by the message of a loving community that did good works in the name of Christ so as to earn the reward of eternal life in heaven. For example, the Book of Revelation is dedicated to seven churches located in Asia Minor, six of which did not exist in Paul's time, including Smyrna (today's Izmir), Pergamum (near today's Bergama); Thyatira (modern Akhisar), Sardis, Philadelphia (today's Alaşehir), and Laodicea (near modern Eskihisar). This underscores the fact that, whereas the Book of Acts largely credits Paul and his disciples with seeding the "churches" of Asia Minor, in reality these early Christian communities coalesced around a number of people who had the means to travel and spread the word of Christ, including sailors, soldiers, officials, and merchants. By the end of the first century, for example, there were around three hundred thousand Christians in Asia Minor alone.

One key factor of this growth was that Christianity was open to all. Unlike other religious sects such as the cult of Isis or Mithras, there was no onerous initiation rite, nor a set of rules that could disqualify a candidate based on his or her race, citizenship, language, or social status. As such, Early Christianity presented a radical repudiation of Roman society and its deeply ingrained class system, which is perhaps why so many Romans considered it subversive. Another factor that greatly facilitated the growth of Early Christianity was the rapid expansion of land and sea routes throughout the empire. Eventually, the Roman highway system would cover some 250,000 miles, of which about 50,000 miles were paved. Under Trajan, no fewer than twenty-nine major highways connected the Roman capital to its Empire. At the same time, there were scheduled nautical routes between the main cities on the Mediterranean. This in turn fostered a growing prosperity that was largely concentrated in the cities—the beginning of European urbanization—which in turn attracted vast numbers of people from surrounding rural territories. All these factors enabled the message of Christ to be carried to the far corners of the Roman Empire at speeds that were unprecedented at any other time. For example, a number of Christian missionaries took the trade routes of Mesopotamia alongside the Tigris and the Euphrates and continued as far the Persian Gulf, and even into India.

By the beginning of the second century, the bishoprics of Rome, Alexandria, and Antioch had emerged as leading centers of Christianity. It was these dioceses that now guided the Christian movement in questions of liturgy, scripture, and practice. Ironically, however, the greatest challenge to Early Christianity did not come from without, but from within. Throughout the first and second centuries, a number of different "Christianities" had begun to emerge and prosper without the direct involvement of either Paul, the Apostles, or members of the communities that they had established. Many of these movements would arrive at a different interpretation of what Jesus was about, based on the oral traditions that were circulating at the time. Some would even believe that Jesus had been a divine being in the Platonic mold, who had come to show his followers how to discover the secret knowledge of God within themselves. Passed on by sages such as the third century CE philosopher Plotinus, Neoplatonism was a philosophy that accepted the existence of the divine, the source of all things, a spark of which was carried in every human being. In fact, a person's soul (*psyché*) could find union with that divine source through a life of virtue and constant reflection, and ultimately find immortality. It therefore did not take a leap of faith to think that there were important parallels between Neoplatonism and Christian ideas. For example, Neoplatonism exerted a powerful influence on the fourth-century theologian Augustine of Hippo.

But the engagement between Christianity and Neoplatonic thought was a double-edged sword, particularly as it related to the understanding of Christ as both human and divine, as a man and a god. Greek philosophers had always had a particular fondness for paradoxes such as this, for it allowed them to plumb the depths of abstract thinking. In the early years of the Christian movement, these contradictions remained in the background while Christianity was fighting for survival and acceptance in the Roman Empire. But that changed after Gallienus, the son and successor of Emperor Valerian, issued a decree of tolerance in the year 259, allowing Christians to build or restore houses of worship and cemeteries. Finally released from any form of persecution, Christian communities throughout the realm launched a vast expansion program, building churches, baptizing converts, and installing bishops. By the end of the third century, there were Christian churches in places as far as Britain, Gaul, and Spain. Even though the decree of tolerance was suspended during the reign of Diocletian, it was reaffirmed by Emperor Constantine in his famous Edict of Milan of 313. According to a legend, Constantine had a dream on the eve of a major battle with a pretender to the throne named Maxentius. He dreamt that he should paint the monogram of Christ, the Greek letters "Chi" and "Rho," on his soldiers' shields. Constantine did so, rode into battle, and defeated Maxentius, crediting the Christian God to his victory.

Epilogue

*Emperor Constantine the Great issued
his decree of religious tolerance in 313.*

Thus secure at last, the Christian movement began to organize itself as a proper "Church." With the active support of
Constantine (who remained a practicing pagan himself), a new
seven-day calendar was promulgated, starting with Sunday as
the *Dies Domini,* or Day of the Lord. A liturgical year was
adopted, regulating the various Christian festivals and feast
days in an annual calendar that culminated in Holy Week and
the most important day of all, Easter. The result was something that Christianity had never enjoyed: an elaborate system
of official sacred rites filled with hymns, readings, and sacra-
ments, many of which are still observed in the Greek Orthodox
Church today.

At the same time, Roman architects began to confront the
need to build houses of worship for the newly licensed Christian

Church. It was soon recognized that the typical design of a Roman temple would not do. The Roman cult placed an emphasis on *individual* worship, with the devout performing a sacrifice in the forecourt before proceeding to the inner sanctum to pray to the god in question. Christian services, on the other hand, required the presence of the entire congregation at one time. What's more, few Christians would have been comfortable with worshipping in a building that had long been associated with polytheism. An entirely new paradigm was needed, an authentic *Christian* temple, which could accommodate hundreds of worshippers. Thus, the choice fell on a Roman building type known as a *basilica,* which heretofore had been used as a civic administration center. From a Christian point of view, the basilica was a perfect choice; it was a secular structure and therefore neutral in a religious sense. Basilicas also featured a semicircular apse to house a statue of the reigning emperor, which could now be used to place the altar.

Given that Constantine the Great had moved the capital of the Roman Empire from the city of Rome to Byzantium, eventually renamed Constantinople (or *Konstantinopolis,* "City of Constantine"), one of the first basilicas to be built was the *Hagia Eiréne,* the church of Holy Peace. After the church burned down in 532, Emperor Justinian had it rebuilt. Remarkably, it still exists today on the grounds of the Topkapi Palace in Istanbul.

Now that Christianity was rapidly becoming a mainstream religion, however, age-old theological issues rose once more to the surface. Gnosticism, rooted in the Greek word *gnōstikos* or "possessing knowledge," is a blend of many different currents that emerged in the late first century CE including Neoplatonism, Zoroastrianism, and various Near Eastern mystery sects. Gnostic Christians believed that the teachings of

| *The basilica of the Hagia Eirene in Istanbul.*

Jesus offered a path to *gnōsis*—a secret knowledge of the divine within themselves. According to their view, Jesus had revealed a deeply intimate way by which humans could communicate directly with God, without the intervention of a priesthood or a set of laws. This explained the need for secrecy, which is why Jesus so often spoke in parables. Some Gnostic factions began to produce their own Gospels, perhaps in response to the emerging New Testament canon of the traditional Church. Many of these are attributed to a noted Apostle so as to bolster their authenticity, including a Gospel of Peter, a Gospel of Philip, and a Gospel of Mary, which exalts Mary Magdalene as an Apostle in her own right. A large cache of these Gnostic Gospels were discovered near Nag Hammadi in Egypt in 1945.

A priest from the Baucalis district of Alexandria, named Arius, thought he had a solution to the intrinsic dilemma of

Jesus' divinity. He argued that while Jesus was divine, his divine substance was subordinate to that of God. Because the Hebrew Bible specified that God created the earth long before he begot Jesus, the two could therefore not be *consubstantial,* of the same substance. Arius based his theory on the Gospel of John, which said that God the Father was always existing, therefore "unbegotten," whereas Jesus, the Son of God, was the "only-begotten" God (John 1:18; 17:3).

The matter may seem obscure to us today, but for the Greek mind it assumed a major significance. Many Christian leaders were alarmed when Arius' ideas—known as *Arianism*—began to rapidly spread through the Christian world, precisely because this solution seemed to settle the nature of Christ's duality. Worse, a number of missionaries who were then trying to convert the barbarian tribes of Western Europe declared their support for Arius as well. This came to the attention of Emperor Constantine, who until now had tried to stay away from these theological debates. The challenge of Arianism, however, compelled him to act. In 325, the emperor summoned 220 bishops to a synod in a town called Nicaea, located near today's city of Iznik in Turkey, in an effort to forge a consensus on the issue. This was a unique development: the idea that a Roman Emperor should preside over a major topic of Christian theology would have been unthinkable at any time during the preceding centuries. It also shows that at this time, it was the secular power of the emperor, rather than the church authority of the major bishoprics, that exercised the greatest influence over the Catholic (i.e., "universal") Church.

The synod at Nicaea debated the issue at length. Was the relationship of Christ to God one of *similar* substance but subordinate, as Arius advocated, or of the *same* substance as the

Catholic faction believed. In Greek, the two terms are so similar (*homoiouson,* "of similar substance" versus *homoousion,* "of the same substance") that the fate of the Church literally hinged on a single letter, an "i" or *iota.* When a final vote was called, the consubstantiality clause won. The resulting "Nicene Creed" is still with us day: "We believe . . . in Jesus Christ, the only Son of God . . . *consubstantial* with the Father" (previously phrased as *"one in Being* with the Father" before the revisions by Pope Benedict XVI).

The triumph was short-lived, however, because the Greek mind could not resist debating this mysterious issue. A different "heresy" known as Monophysitism argued that Christ had always been divine to begin with. In the fifth century, the Archbishop of Constantinople, Nestorius, articulated an opposite view, that Jesus represented two natures, both human and divine, which coexisted in the incarnate Christ. The result was a movement called Nestorianism that was loudly denounced in Constantinople proper, but rapidly gained ground elsewhere. Using Sassanid Persia as its base, Nestorianism was astonishingly successful in building a "Church of the East" in Asia, absorbing the early Christian settlements of India and reaching as far as China during the Tang Dynasty. In fact, by the ninth century the "Church of the East" (or the "East Syriac Church") had geographically speaking become the largest Christian movement of its time, stretching from Mesopotamia and Persia to India and China.

By this time also, two major power blocs had emerged in the Church: the Byzantine Church led by the patriarch of Constantinople, and the European Church governed by the pope in Rome. Culturally, they were different as well: Byzantium still clung to the Greek language and Greek rites, whereas the dominant liturgical language in Europe was Latin. The Eastern Church believed that West European Christianity was crude and unsophisticated, lacking the learning of the clergy in Constantinople, whereas the West mocked the heresies that kept popping up in the Eastern Church. In 1054, matters came to a head when Pope Leo IX appointed an archbishop in Sicily, which the Byzantine Church claimed as its own jurisdiction. In retaliation, Patriarch Michael Cerularius of Constantinople ordered the closing of all Latin churches in the Byzantine capital. Soon thereafter, the split between the Greek and Latin Churches became final—a split that continues to this day in the tensions between the Greek Orthodox Church and the Roman Catholic Church.

But worse was to come. In the West, a rift was developing between the secular powers of Europe and the pope in Rome. The source of this conflict, surprisingly, were the Crusades. From a purely military point of view, the Crusades were a failure. Only the First Crusade succeeded in establishing four Christian "kingdoms" in Palestine, but within less than a century all succumbed to Muslim conquests under Salah-ad-Din (known as Saladin to the West). From a historical perspective, however, the impact of the Crusades was more keenly felt in Europe itself than on the battlefields of the Middle East. By organizing these expeditions, Europe's nobility marshalled military and economic resources that had lain dormant since the fall of the Roman Empire in the West. Thus was born the outline of a modern Europe, with true nation states that recognized their unique cultural and economic manifest destiny. Together, their leaders nominated one august person to hold the most important title of all: that of Holy Roman Emperor, a title once held by the legendary eighth-century king Charlemagne.

Epilogue

This development produced the so-called Investiture Conflict, which asked the question: who is the ultimate authority of Latin Christianity, the pope or the Holy Roman Emperor? Though this question was never settled to the satisfaction of all, it inspired a long rivalry in the twelfth and thirteenth centuries between rural towns that pledged their fealty to the pope, known as the Guelph party, and mercantile cities that supported the emperor, known as the Ghibellines.

The conflict between the religious and secular powers of Europe came to a head in the greatest crisis in Christianity: the Reformation. In 1521, the Catholic Church stood at the zenith of its power. But the papacy had become subject to intense rivalries between the Italian houses of the Rovere, the Borgia, and the Medici. Worse, these popes professed little interest in religious matters or the wellbeing of their flock. Instead, they devoted themselves to sensuous pursuits, such as the hosting of lavish banquets and masques, the creation of magnificent works of art, or the raising of troops to conquer territory for the Papal States. All this required a lot of money, of course, particularly when Pope Julius II launched his most ambitious project: the completion of a new St. Peter's Basilica in Rome. The scheme continued under Pope Leo X, who in his search for new sources of funding focused on the sale of indulgences. These offered the bearer (or whomever one designates as the beneficiary) a respite from the time spent in purgatory. The Catholic clergy taught that purgatory was some sort of a halfway house, a probationary state between death and heaven, with rather uncomfortable facilities.

The practice enraged an Augustinian monk called Martin Luther, who was serving as a member of the faculty at the University of Wittenberg. Luther strongly believed that no man, neither priest nor pope, could promise relief from purgatory. The reason was that no human being had the power to forgive sins. Only God could do that. What was needed, Luther believed, was a total reform of the Mother Church to cleanse it of these practices and return it to the spiritual message of the Gospels. This was the thrust of a document that he nailed to the door of the castle church at Wittenberg in 1517, known as the *Ninety-Five Theses*. Indulgences were not the only target of Luther's wrath. He also denounced the exploitation of gullible pilgrims who flocked to Saxony to see the largest concentration of relics in all of Europe.

Luther was not alone; other intellectuals had called for a reform of the Church, including Thomas à Kempis, John Wycliffe, and the Dutch humanist Erasmus, but Luther's initiative succeeded beyond all expectations. Aided by a new invention called the printing press, his *Theses* spread through Europe like wildfire. The result was a growing force that no longer contemplated a reform of the Catholic Church, but rather sought to create a new movement, a *Lutheran* church in German lands, no longer governed by the bishop of Rome.[2] When in 1526 the rulers of the 300-odd German states were given a choice for either Catholicism or Lutheranism, a majority chose to create an indigenous Lutheran Church, albeit for political rather than purely religious reasons.

As the Reformation spread, other movements sprang up, including one inspired by the French theologian John Calvin, who fled to Geneva, Switzerland to organize the movement known as Calvinism. This movement also spread to France, where its followers became known as *Huguenots*. When the English King Henry VIII tried to set aside his consort, the Spanish Queen Catherine, in favor of Anne Boleyn and Pope

Clement VII refused to grant him an annulment, the King made himself head of the newly formed Church of England, which eventually developed into the Anglican Church.

And so, by the end of the sixteenth century, the great Christian movement had succumbed to a number of splits and schisms that would continue to develop in the centuries to come. By the dawn of the twenty-first century, there were forty thousand different Christian denominations around the world, and more than two hundred denominations in the United States alone.

In the process, the core idea of Christians as people following the words of Jesus has often been lost. As a result of our nation's culture wars, Christianity has become a matter of taking sides, of being *for* something or *against* something. This is largely the outcome of various Church teachings that emerged over the centuries, but that in recent decades have been exploited by politicians to divide the Christian community.

But that is not what Jesus was about. What he was about was *love*. Pure, simple, unadulterated love for every human being: man or woman, young or old, Black, brown or white. As a man of color, a son of Galilee with olive-colored skin, he had experienced prejudice himself, and strenuously argued that such had no place in the Kingdom of God. Instead, he envisioned the Kingdom as a domain where people could feel safe, be respected, and live their lives in dignity to the fullest, regardless of their station or condition. When a scribe asked him to name the most important commandment, Jesus quoted the *Shema* from Deuteronomy 6:5: "you shall love the Lord your God with all your heart and with all your soul and with all your mind and with all your strength," and then cited the second commandment: "You shall love your neighbor as yourself," adding,

"There is no other commandment greater than these" (Mark 12:30–31).

Why is that so difficult to understand, when Jesus pounds away at his Kingdom concept time and again, parable after parable, sermon after sermon? Why don't we talk about *that* for a change, rather than engaging in our culture wars? Like many of you, I was shocked to learn that some gun manufacturers, like Trijicon, engraved their AR-15 machine guns with quotes from the Bible, as if that would make these weapons an acceptable attribute of Christians.[3] In all his teachings, Jesus emphasizes the absolute rejection of any form of violence, or the means to commit violence. On the night of his arrest, when Peter was ready to defend Jesus with his sword, Jesus responded, "Put your sword back in its place. . . for all who draw the sword will die by the sword" (Matthew 26:52). What could be clearer than that? If Peter had been carrying a rifle, Jesus would have said the same thing.

It is not that Jesus was blind to the evil that exists in the world. As we saw, the ancient world in which he lived was filled with sources of evil, as is ours today. But he made the point that evil begins in our hearts. "Listen to me, all of you, and understand," Jesus said; "there is nothing outside a person that by going in can defile, but the things that come out are what defile. . . . For it is from within, from the human heart, that evil intentions come: sexual exploitation, theft, murder, adultery, avarice, wickedness, deceit, debauchery, envy, slander, pride, folly. All these evil things come from within, and they defile a person" (Mark 7:14–23). Of course, this particular discourse was to some extent directed at the Pharisees, and their obsession with the purity of things that people touch, drink, or eat. But the deeper meaning is that as long as evil exists in the world, we must combat evil with love, and not allow those with evil intent to acquire the means to do us harm. "Blessed are the peacemakers," Jesus said, "for they will be called children of God" (Matthew 5:9).

The first commandment, to love God with all your heart and all your soul and all your mind, is just as important. But for us, in the twenty-first century, that type of spirituality has become a challenge as well. As I wrote in my book *The Search for Heaven,* we have lost the art of being alone with ourselves. Whenever we pause for a moment, like waiting for a red light or standing in an elevator, we whip out our smartphones to check the latest Twitter or Instagram feed. That modern instinct has made it very difficult for us to pause and experience genuine spirituality. But it doesn't need to be. To find a moment in the day to be spiritual, to pray or meditate, is a wonderful opportunity to separate ourselves from our physical needs and to search for the voice of the Divine in ourselves. That is exactly why, when Jesus refers to God as his *Abba,* he encourages us to do the same thing. Calling God *Abba* was not his privilege alone, but available to all who follow him. This idea is enshrined in the prayer that forms the core of this book, which begins with the words, "*Our* Father." God is the father of us all. Only when we as a people choose this path, only when we act justly with one another, will the deep social chasms of our world be bridged. That is the ultimate purpose of Jesus' Kingdom—to be a nation of children of God, living together in harmony.

CHRONOLOGY

BEFORE THE COMMON ERA (BCE)

166 BCE   Judea, a province of the Seleucid Empire, rises in revolt against Antiochus IV Epiphanes (175–163 BCE). The rebellion is led by brothers of the Maccabeus family (hence the term "Maccabean Revolt"), which will ultimately establish the Hasmonean dynasty.

152   Antiochus' successor, Demetrius I, appoints Jonathan Maccabeus as governor of Judea in a first step to Judean independence.

150   Jonathan also assumes the position of high priest. Many pious Jews (*Hasidim*) are dismayed by the Hasmonean usurpation of this position, which is traditionally reserved for descendants of Solomon's priest Zadok.

HASMONEAN ERA

142   Jonathan is killed. His brother Simeon succeeds him as king and high priest and secures Judean independence. Control over the Sanhedrin (the Jewish Great Council with considerable legislative and judicial power) is contested by two parties: the conservative, priestly-aristocratic Sadducees and the more progressive brotherhood known as the Pharisees.

103   Under the Hasmonean king Alexander Jannaeus (103–76 BCE), Judea is increasingly Hellenized (shaped by the cultural influence of Ancient Greece). Alexander also expands his kingdom by incorporating Galilee and parts of the Transjordan and coastal regions. A falling-out with Pharisees leads to the destruction of the Pharisaic party as a political force. The Sadducees take control of the Sanhedrin.

76   Alexander is succeeded by his wife, queen Salome Alexandra (76–67 BCE), who restores many Pharisees in key positions.

67   The death of Queen Alexandra plunges the Hasmonean kingdom into civil war, with Alexander's sons, Hyrcanus II and Aristobulus II, vying for the throne.

ROMAN ERA

63   The Roman general Pompey intervenes in the Judean civil war and establishes Palestine as a vassal state of Rome, led by Hyrcanus II as puppet king. Soon thereafter, an Idumean nobleman called Antipater is appointed governor (*epitropos*) of Judea, serving under Hyrcanus.

47   Antipater's son Herod is appointed governor (*strategos*) of Galilee. With Roman auxiliary forces, Herod is able to suppress a rebellion led by a Galilean named Hezekiah. Herod also ravages the Galilean countryside to raise funds on behalf of Cassius, one of the assassins of Julius Caesar.

40   Parthians invade Judea, ostensibly in support of Antigonus, the son of Aristobulus II, and oust Hyrcanus and Antipater. Herod flees to Rome, where he persuades the Senate to declare him king of all Palestine.

39   Herod lands in Palestine backed by Roman forces, conquers the country, and besieges Jerusalem. In 37, Jerusalem is captured, and Antigonus is killed. The reign of King Herod the Great (37–4 BCE) begins.

HERODIAN RULE

30   Octavian, known as Augustus since 27 BCE, is confirmed as Roman emperor. Herod begins the construction of a vast harbor in Caesarea and builds a new city near the ancient site of Samaria, known as Sebaste, dedicated to Augustus (*Sebastos* in Greek).

22   In an attempt to curry favor with his Jewish subjects, Herod begins a vast expansion of the Second Temple in Jerusalem, which is not completed until 62 CE. To finance this and other large construction projects, Herod lays a heavy tax yoke on the peasantry of Judea and Galilee. Herod also imports priestly families from Persia to create a line of high priests whose loyalty to the Herodian dynasty is unquestioned.

5–4   Putative date of birth of Jesus, son of Joseph and Mary.

4   Herod dies. His will proposes a division of his kingdom among his sons. Herod's son Archelaus, who is granted the largest share of Judea and Samaria, faces increasing protests over the heavy tax burden. Archelaus responds with a brutal military suppression, then leaves for Rome.

4   A son of the defeated rebel leader Hezekiah, named Judas, leads a new rebellion in Galilee. All resistance is brutally repressed by Roman legions dispatched from Antioch, capital of Roman Syria. Galilee is ravaged. The Galilean city of Sepphoris is burned to the ground.

4   Roman emperor Augustus accepts Herod's will and confirms Archelaus as *ethnarch* of Judea and Samaria; Herod's son Antipas as *tetrarch* of Galilee and Perea, and Herod's son Philip as *tetrarch* of Gaulanitis, Batanea, and Trachonitis.

THE COMMON ERA (CE)

6 CE   Archelaus is removed from office because of his misrule and banished to Vienne in Roman Gaul. Augustus turns Judea into a Roman province, to be led by a prefect reporting to the Roman governor in Antioch, Syria. That governor, Quirinius, initiates a census in Judea to determine the tax value of the new province.

6   The Roman census leads to a widespread civil disobedience campaign in Palestine led by "Judas the Galilean."

6–10   Antipas (also known as Herod Antipas) begins the rebuilding of Sepphoris, using a Greco-Roman city plan.

14   Emperor Augustus dies and is succeeded by Tiberius (14–37 CE).

20   Herod Antipas suspends the construction of Sepphoris and decides to build a new Hellenistic city on the Sea of Galilee, called Tiberias (dedicated to emperor Tiberius).

26   Pontius Pilatus (known as Pilate) arrives in Caesarea to begin his term as prefect of the Roman province of Judea. He provokes popular outrage by placing army insignia carrying the portrait of the emperor near the Temple precinct in Jerusalem, violating the Jewish law against "graven images."

28   The Aqueduct Affair once again leads to massive protests against Pilate. Hundreds of demonstrators in Jerusalem are brutally cut down by Roman soldiers hidden among the crowd.

28 (?)   Jesus joins the movement of John the Baptist in the Jordan wilderness. At some later date, John is arrested by Antipas.

28 (?)   After John's arrest, Jesus and a small group of other Galilean followers of John flee north, possibly to Bethsaida.

28–29   Beginning of the ministry of Jesus in Galilee.

30 (?)   Jesus and his followers go to Jerusalem to visit the Temple during the Passover festival. Jesus stages a disturbance in the Temple. He is arrested, indicted by a group of Sadducees led by the high priest Caiaphas, and transferred into the custody of the Roman governor for execution. Jesus is crucified on the charge of having plotted sedition against the Roman occupation. According to the Gospels, after three days he is raised from the dead.

30–35 (?) Jewish followers of Jesus, now led by Jesus' brother James, are increasingly marginalized in Judea. One follower,

Stephen, is stoned to death by a mob, which includes Saul of Tarsus.

30–35 (?) Saul halts his persecution of Jewish Christians and joins the movement. Before the beginning of his first missionary journey, he changes his name to the Latinized *Paulus* or "Paul."

36 Pilate is removed from office because of his excessive cruelty. At the same time, Caiaphas is removed from his post as high priest.

37 Agrippa I, a grandson of Herod the Great, is appointed king of Judea.

39 Herod Antipas, ruler of Galilee, is removed from office by the Roman emperor Gaius ("Caligula") and exiled to Lugdunum (Lyon) in Roman Gaul.

44 King Herod Agrippa dies; Judea reverts to being a Roman province.

45–46 (?) The "Jerusalem Conference" leads to a split between James and Paul. The church of James continues to focus its activity on observant Jews in Palestine, while Paul concentrates on converting Gentiles (as well as Jews) in Asia Minor and Greece.

45–50 Possible date for the text of Jesus sayings known as "Q" (*Quelle,* or "source").

53–57 Paul and his associates write his principal *oeuvre* of letters (including epistles to the Galatians, Corinthians, and Romans).

62 James is condemned by members of the Sanhedrin under the auspices of the high priest Ananus ben Ananus and stoned to death.

64	Putative date for the deaths of Peter and Paul in Rome, following the Great Fire in that city and Nero's decision to blame it on Rome's Christian community.
60–65	Putative date of the source text of the "Gospel of Thomas."
66	Growing resentment of corrupt Roman prefects precipitates the outbreak of a nationwide Jewish rebellion against Roman rule, known as the First Jewish War.
67	The Roman general Vespasian lands in Syria to take command of the war against the Jewish rebellion.
69	Vespasian is declared emperor by his troops. The prosecution of the war against the remnants of the Jewish rebellion is taken over by his son Titus.
70	Titus captures Jerusalem, effectively ending the Jewish War (though pockets of resistance in the Dead Sea area are not defeated until 73–74). The Second Temple is destroyed, marking the end of Second Temple Judaism.
ca. 66–70	The author known as Mark writes his Gospel, possibly in Rome.
75	Josephus completes his book *The Jewish War* in Rome.
ca. 75–85	The author known as Matthew writes his Gospel.
ca. 75–85	The author known as Luke writes his Gospel.
93	Josephus completes his book *Antiquities of the Jews* in Rome.
ca. 85–95	The author known as John writes his Gospel.
ca. 95	Putative date of the book *Antiquities of the Jews* by Josephus.
132	Outbreak of Second Jewish War, known as the Bar Kokhba Revolt.

135	Emperor Hadrian razes Jerusalem and builds a new city, Aelia Capitolina, in its place.
ca. 185	Bishop Irenaeus proposes an anthology of the Gospels of Matthew, Mark, Luke, and John as the canon of Christianity.
261	Emperor Gallienus ends persecution of Christians.
313	Constantine the Great issues Edict of Milan, tolerating all religions in the Roman Empire including Christianity.
ca. 320	A priest named Arius argues that while Jesus was divine, his divine substance was subordinate to that of God. This idea would inspire a movement called Arianism.
325	Opening of the Council of Nicaea which rules against Arianism and instead articulates the Nicene creed that Jesus is "consubstantial" with God the Father.
331	Capital of the Roman Empire is formally moved to Constantinople.
389	Emperor Theodosius issues decree criminalizing worship of any religion other than Christianity.
431	During the Council of Ephesus, Nestorius is deposed as patriarch of Constantinople because of his teachings that Jesus represented two natures, both human and divine, a movement called Nestorianism.
451	The Council of Chalcedon leads to a break between the Catholic Church and the "non-Chalcedonian" Churches, which support the Monophysite doctrine, which argues that Christ had always been a divine being.
537	The new church of the Hagia Sophia in Constantinople is consecrated.
550	The crucifix emerges as a major church ornament.

614	More than 65,000 Christians are killed in the Persian conquest of Jerusalem.
630	All of Arabia is unified under the banner of Islam.
638	Muslim Caliph Umar ibn al-Khattab conquers the Holy Land.
812	Constantinople recognizes Charlemagne as Holy Roman Emperor in the West.
ca. 835	The "Church of the East" (or the "East Syriac Church") is geographically speaking the largest Christian territory of its time, stretching from Mesopotamia and Persia to India and China.
912	Umayyad nobleman Abd-al-Rahman III initiates the period of the Convivencia in Muslim Spain.
1054	The Great Schism splits Christianity into the Eastern Orthodox and Roman Catholic Churches.
1096	First Crusade to liberate the Holy Land from Muslim rule begins.
1099	Beginning of the 88-year Crusader rule of the Holy Land.
1187	Salah-ad-Din defeats Crusader forces at the Battle of Hattin.
1204	Constantinople is sacked by militia of the Fourth Crusade.
1245	Pope Innocent IV strips Frederick II of the title of Holy Roman Emperor.
1260	The Florentine Ghibellines defeat the papal Guelphs at Montaperti.
1309	The papal court of Clement V moves to Avignon, where it will remain for the next 70 years.
1368	The Ming Dynasty outlaws Christianity in China.

1378	The election of the Italian Pope Urban VI prompts French cardinals to elect Clement VII; soon, three claimants compete for the throne of St. Peter.
1439	The Byzantine patriarch, Joseph, signs a formal treaty of reunification between the Greek and Latin Churches.
1440	The reunification treaty is repudiated by Constantinople.
1492	Christopher Columbus sails on his voyage to the New World.
1516	Johann Tetzel, a Dominican friar, offers indulgences for sale in Germany.
1517	Martin Luther nails a copy of his *95 Theses* on the castle church at Wittenberg.
1526	The majority of German rulers adopt Lutheranism.
1534	The Act of Supremacy declares Henry VIII to be the supreme head of the Church of England.
1539	John Calvin completes his tract *Institutes of the Christian Religion*, launching Calvinism.
1545	The Council of Trent redefines Catholicism and launches the Counter-Reformation.
1559	John Knox begins the Protestant Reformation of Scotland.
1596	The Swedish Church formally adopts the Augsburg Confession to become Lutheran.
1607	The Jamestown settlement is the first permanent English colony in the New World.

FURTHER READING

The Second Temple Period

Mark A. Chancey, *The Myth of a Gentile Galilee.* Cambridge University Press, 2002.

K.C. Hanson and Douglas E. Oakman, *Palestine in the Time of Jesus: Social Structures and Social Conflicts.* Fortress Press, 1998.

Daniel Harrington, *The Maccabean Revolt: Anatomy of a Biblical Revolution.* Michael Glazier, 1991.

W. D. Davies, L. Finkelstein (eds.), *The Cambridge History of Judaism*, Vols. 1–3. Cambridge University Press, 1999.

Israel Finkelstein, and Amihai Mazar, *The Quest for the Historical Israel.* Society of Biblical Literature, 2007

Jack Finnegan, *The Archaeology of the New Testament.* Princeton University Press, 1992

Richard Horsley, *Galilee: History, Politics, People.* Trinity Press, 1995.

Jean-Pierre Isbouts, *The Biblical World: An Illustrated Atlas.* National Geographic Society, 2007.

Jodi Magness, *Stone and Dung, Oil and Spit: Jewish Life in the Time of Jesus*. Eerdmans, 2011.

Jodi Magness, *The Archaeology of the Holy Land, from the Destruction of Solomon's Temple to the Muslim Conquest*. Cambridge University Press, 2012.

Jacob Neusner, *Judaism When Christianity Began: A Survey of Belief and Practice*. John Knox Press, 2002.

Jonathan L. Reed, *The HarperCollins Visual Guide to the New Testament*. HarperCollins, 2007.

Neil Asher Silberman and David B. Small, *The Archeology of Israel: Constructing the Past, Interpreting the Present*. Sheffield Academic Press, 1997.

Merrill C. Tenney, *New Testament Times*. Hendrickson Publishers, 2001.

Fabian E. Udoh, *To Caesar What Is Caesar's: Tribute, Taxes, and Imperial Administration in Early Roman Palestine (63 B.C.E.–70 C.E.)*. Brown Judaic Studies, 2005.

Jesus

James K. Beilby and Paul Rhodes Eddy (eds.), *The Historical Jesus: Five Views*. InterVarsity Press, 2009.

Marcus J. Borg, *Jesus: Uncovering the Life, Teachings, and Relevance of a Religious Revolutionary*. HarperSanFrancisco, 2006.

Bruce Chilton, *Rabbi Jesus*. Doubleday, 2000.

John Dominic Crossan, *The Historical Jesus: The Life of a Mediterranean Jewish Peasant*. HarperSanFrancisco, 1991.

John Dominic Crossan, *Jesus: A Revolutionary Biography*. HarperCollins, 1994.

John Dominic Crossan, and Jonathan L. Reed, *Excavating Jesus: Beneath the Stones, behind the Texts*. HarperCollins, 2001.

Further Reading

Craig Evans, *Jesus and His World: The Archaeological Evidence.* Westminster John Knox Press, 2012.

William R. Herzog II, *Parables as Subversive Speech: Jesus as Pedagogue of the Oppressed.* Westminster/John Knox Press, 1994.

Richard Horsley, *Jesus and the Spiral of Violence: Popular Jewish Resistance in Roman Palestine.* Fortress Press, 1993.

Richard Horsley, *Jesus and Empire: The Kingdom of God and the New World Disorder.* Fortress Press, 2003.

Jean-Pierre Isbouts, *In the Footsteps of Jesus: A Chronicle of his Life and the Origins of Christianity.* National Geographic Society, 2012

Barbara Levick, *Tiberius the Politician.* Routledge, 2005.

Amy-Jill Levine (ed.), *Historical Jesus in Context.* Princeton University Press, 2006.

Byron R. McCane, *Roll Back the Stone: Death and Burial in the World of Jesus.* Trinity Press International, 2003.

John P. Meier, *A Marginal Jew: Rethinking the Historical Jesus,* Vols. 1–5. Yale University Press, 2016.

Donald Senior, *Jesus: A Gospel Portrait.* Paulist Press, 1992.

John E. Stambaugh and David L. Balch, *The New Testament in Its Social Environment.* The Westminster Press, 1986.

Gerd Theissen and Annette Merz, *The Historical Jesus: A Comprehensive Guide.* Fortress Press, 1998.

Ian Wilson, *Jesus: The Evidence.* Phoenix Illustrated, 1998.

N.T. Wright, *Jesus and the Victory of God.* Fortress Press, 1996.

Ann Wroe, *Pilate: The Biography of an Invented Man.* Vintage, 2000.

Source Documents

Richard Bauckham, *Jesus and the Eyewitnesses: The Gospels as Eyewitness Testimony.* William B. Eerdmans Publishing Company, 2006.

Roy B. Blizzard, *Mishnah and the Words of Jesus.* CreateSpace, 2013.

Robert Cargill, *Qumran Through (Real) Time: A Virtual Reconstruction of Qumran.* Gorgias Press, 2009.

Herbert Danby, *The Mishnah: Translated from the Hebrew with Introduction and Brief Explanatory Notes.* Hendrickson Academic, 2012.

Jean-Pierre Isbouts, *The Dead Sea Scrolls: 75 Years since their Historic Discovery.* National Geographic Society, 2021.

Rudolphe Kasser, Marvin Meyer, and Gregor Wurst, *The Gospel of Judas.* National Geographic Society, 2008.

Amy-Jill Levine and Marc Zvi Brettler, *The Jewish Annotated New Testament.* Oxford University Press, 2011.

Burton L. Mack, *Q: The Lost Gospel.* HarperSanFrancisco, 1993.

Paul L. Maier, *Josephus: The Essential Works.* Kregel Publications, 1995.

Jacob Neusner, *The Mishnah: An Introduction.* Rowman & Littlefield Publishers, Inc., 2004.

Elaine Pagels, *Beyond Belief: The Secret Gospel of Thomas.* Random House, 2003.

Elaine Pagels, *The Gnostic Gospels.* Random House, 2004.

J. M. Robinson (ed.), *The Nag Hammadi Library.* E. J. Brill, 1977.

Lawrence H. Schiffman, *Reclaiming the Dead Sea Scrolls: The History of Judaism, the Background of Christianity, the Lost Library of Qumran.* Doubleday, 1995.

William Whiston, *The New Complete Works of Josephus, with Commentary by Paul L. Maier.* Thomas Nelson, 2003.

Michael Wise, Martin Abegg Jr., and Edward Cook (eds.), *The Dead Sea Scrolls: A New Translation.* HarperOne, 2005.

Matthew Wilson, *The Gnostic Gospels: The Gnostic Wisdom of Jesus including the Lost Apocryphal Gospel of Thomas, John and Mary Magdalene.* History Academy, 2021.

Early Christianity

Bruce Chilton, *Rabbi Paul: An Intellectual Biography.* Image/ Doubleday, 2005.

Craig A. Evans (ed.), *The World of Jesus and the Early Church.* Hendrickson Publishers, 2011.

James D. G. Dunn (ed.), *The Cambridge Companion to St. Paul.* Cambridge University Press, 2003.

Bart Ehrman, *Lost Christianities: The Battles for Scripture and the Faiths We Never Knew.* Oxford University Press, 2003.

Jas Elsner, *Imperial Rome and Christian Triumph.* New York: Oxford University Press, 1998.

Jean-Pierre Isbouts, *The Story of Christianity.* National Geographic Society, 2014.

Mullin, Robert B., *A Short World History of Christianity.* Westminster John Knox Press, 2008.

NOTES

Introduction

1. Charlton Heston and Jean-Pierre Isbouts, *Charlton Heston's Hollywood.* pp. 122–124.

2. *The Economist*/YouGov.com, October 29 - November 1, 2022.

3. See Isbouts, Jean-Pierre, *The Story of Christianity.* National Geographic Society, 2014.

4. See Isbouts, Jean-Pierre and Asbury, Neal, *Mapping America.* Apollo Publishers, 2021.

5. Douthat, Ross, "Joe Biden's Catholic Moment," in *The New York Times,* January 23, 2021.

6. See Gallup.com: https://news.gallup.com/opinion/polling-matters/324410/religious-group-voting-2020-election.aspx

1. A Land in Crisis

1. As its wealth increased, the North (or "Israel") began to build a centralized administrative structure that, by the mid-ninth century, became a "state" in the true sense of the word. This northern state, however, was governed not from Galilee but from its neighboring region to the south. Here, on a summit in the hills of Ephraim, just northwest of Shechem, king

Omri chose a spot for a new capital. He called it Samaria, "after the name of Shemer, the owner of the hill" (1 Kings 16:24). The site overlooked the road that linked the Transjordan and the King's Highway with the coastal trade routes along the Mediterranean—including those leading to the port city of Tyre. Today, the remains of Samaria are still visible just outside the village of Sebastiya, some eight miles north of Nablus.

2. See Gal, Zvi, "Israel in Exile: Deserted Galilee testifies to Assyrian Conquest of the Northern Kingdom," in *Biblical Archaeology Review,* Vol. 24:03, May/June 1998.

3. "Galilee of the Gentiles" and similar designations appear in Isaiah 9:1 (LXX Isaiah 8:23); LXX Joel 4:4, 1 Maccabees 5:15, and Matthew 4:15.

4. Josephus, *Against Apion,* 1.60

5. M.I. Finley, *The Ancient Economy.* University of California Press, 1999; p. 105. The Romans called the amount of land a man could plow in a day a *jugum*, the unit by which they measured the size of a man's holdings.

6. Quoted from a 1997 UN survey, in: Hudson-Rodd, Nancy, *Housing, Land, and Property Rights in Burma.* Centre for Housing Rights and Evictions (COHRE), 2004.

7. Richard Horsley, *Galilee: History, Politics, People.* Trinity Press, 1995; pp. 217–219.

8. Sanders, E.P., *The Historical Figure of Jesus.* Penguin, 1996; pp. 146–169.

9. Josephus, *Antiquities* XV. 365–369.

10. Josephus, *Antiquities* XVII. 810.

2. The Lost Years of Jesus' Youth

1. Bruce Hilton, *Rabbi Jesus: An Intimate Biography.* Doubleday, 2000.

2. Josephus, *Antiquities,* XVII.9 §3

3. Josephus, *Antiquities,* XVII.10 §5

4. Josephus, *Antiquities,* XVII.13 §2

5. Josephus, *Antiquities,*XIV.414, *Jewish War* I.304.

6. Jesus' brother James would later become the leader of the Jesus movement in Jerusalem.

7. Significantly, Sepphoris refused to come to the aid of the Second Temple in Jerusalem when the Romans drew near. Josephus, *Vita,* 348.

8. Q 19, which according to Burton Mack belongs to some of the oldest sayings traditions about Jesus. Mack, Burton L., *The Lost Gospel: The Book of Q and Christian Origins.* HarperCollins, 1993.

9. Source: Mayo Clinic, Rochester, Minnesota.

10. Garnsey, Peter, *Cities, Peasants and Food in Classical Antiquity.* University of Cambridge Press, 2009; p. 240.

11. "Malnutrition." *World Health Organization*, April 15, 2020. https://www.who.int/news-room/questions-and-answers/item/malnutrition, retrieved December 13, 2022.

12. Fernandez, I., Himes, J., & de Onis, M., "Prevalence of nutritional wasting in populations." *Bulletin of the World Health Organization*, 80(4):282–91.

13. Mora, J., Gueri, M., & Mora, O., "Vitamin A Deficiency in Latin America and the Caribbean: An overview." *Rev Panam Salud Publica*, 1998 Sep; 4(3):178–86.

14. Garnsey, Peter, *Cities, Peasants and Food in Classical Antiquity*; Ch. 14.

15. Cahill, Jane, Reinhard, K. and Tarler, D., Warnock, P., "It Had to Happen: Archaeologists Examine Remains of Ancient Bathroom." *Biblical Archaeology Review* 17/3: 64–69.

3. Along the Banks of the Jordan

1. Psalms of Solomon XVIII:6–8.

2. We can only imagine what the total take from all the Jewish communities in the far-flung Diaspora would have amounted to. Indeed, after the turmoil surrounding the death of Herod the Great, the Romans were able to steal more than four hundred talents (the equivalent of some 9.6 million sesterces) from the Temple treasury.

3. Habakkuk Pescher 7:4.

4. Scholarship is divided over the question whether this Philip was Antipas' brother Philip, Tetrarch of the Gaulanities, or Herod Philip I.

5. Josephus, *Antiquities,* XVIII.5 §2

4. Jesus Launches His Ministry

1. Both Hollenbach and Sanders have tried to link accounts of demonic possession to the incidence of mental illness in Roman-occupied Palestine. Hollenbach states that "the colonial situation of domination and revolution nourishes mental illness in extraordinary numbers of the population," and suggests that demonic possession was actually a "socially acceptable form of oblique protest against, or escape from, oppressions." Hollenbach, P.W., "Jesus, demoniacs, and public authorities: A socio-historical study," in: *Journal of the American Academy of Religion*, 1981: p. 575. Sanders, furthermore, has argued that Jesus' exorcisms challenged the ruling political and religious authorities for his apparent ability to control demonic powers and attract huge crowds in the process. Sanders, E.P., *Jesus and Judaism*, 1985: p. 173.

2. The segment reads: "Woe is me because of the house of Boethus, woe is me because of their staves!/Woe is me because of the house of Hanin, woe is me because of their whisperings!/Woe is me because of the house of Kathros, woe is me because of their pens!/Woe is me because of the house of Ishmail the son of Phabi, woe is me because of their fists!/"For they are high priests and their sons are (Temple) treasurers and their sons-in-law are trustees and their servants beat the people with staves," in: B. Pesach 57a. See also Fiensy, David A., *The Social History of Palestine in the Herodian Period*. Edwin Mellen Publishers, 1991; pp. 51–52.

3. Josephus, *Jewish War*, II.17 §6

4. Martin Buber, *On Judaism: An Introduction to the Essence of Judaism*. Schocken, 1996; p.122.

5. The fact that Jesus dines with sinners, says Patrick Mullen in a study, "challenges the [Pharisees] to inclusivity and humble honesty, and to recognition of their own need for forgiveness." Mullen, J. Patrick, *Dining with Pharisees*. Liturgical Press, 2004; p. 125.

6. The saying is sometimes considered a paraphrase of Proverbs 25:6–7: "Do not put yourself forward in the king's presence or stand in the place of the great, for it is better to be told, 'Come up here,' than to be put lower in the presence of a noble."

7. See, for example, William R. Herzog II, *Parables as Subversive Speech*. Westminster/John Knox Press, 1994.

8. Aramaic reconstruction by Steve Caruso.

9. Sinclair Bugeja, *An Exegetical Study of the Lord's Prayer as found in the Gospels according to Matthew and Luke.* University of Malta, Faculty of Theology; June, 2015.

5. *Our Father, Hallowed Be Your Name*

1. Mishnah Yebamot 4:13.

2. Birmingham, George A., *Jeremiah the Prophet*; New York: Harper & Brothers, 1939; p. 31.

6. *Your Kingdom Come*

1. Strabo, *Geography*, 14:5,1.

2. Statista Research Department, October 11, 2022.

3. Dottie Rosenbaum and Zoë Neuberger, "President's 2021 Budget Would Cut Food Assistance for Millions and Radically Restructure SNAP." *Center on Budget and Policy Priorities*, February 18, 2020.

4. Jennifer Tolbert, Patrick Drake, and Anthony Damico, "Key Facts about the Uninsured Population." *Kaiser Family Foundation*, December 19, 2022.

7. *Give Us Each Day Our Bread*

1. Safrai, Ze'ev, *The Economy of Roman Palestine*, p. 105.

2. I am indebted to several books and articles by Miriam Feinberg Vamosh in which she has described the Pesach meal as it would have been cooked and served in first-century Palestine.

3. Mishnah Pesachim, 10.1.

4. Mishnah Pesachim 1.

5. https://www.ers.usda.gov/topics/food-nutrition-assistance/food-security-in-the-u-s/key-statistics-graphics/, retrieved November 23, 2022.

8. *And Forgive Us Our Debts*

1. Another Aramaic translation of Scripture was reportedly compiled by Jonathan ben Uzziel, a disciple of the great Jewish sage Hillel (who was active 30–10 BCE).

2. It appears that in the translation from the Hebrew to the Aramaic Bible, the same problems emerged with regards to translating the double meaning of debts/sins. For example, in the Hebrew Torah, Pharaoh says to Moses, "Do forgive my sin this once" (Exodus 10:17). The Aramaic Targum, however, translates this as follows: "Remit my debt just this once" (TgExod 10:17).

9. *And Do Not Bring Us to the Test*

1. John Yieh, "Lord's Prayer" in *The New Interpreter's Dictionary of the Bible*. Abingdon Press, 2009; p. 695.
2. In fact, the Qumran sect and John the Baptist lived in close proximity to one another—the Qumranites on the northwestern shore of the Dead Sea and the Baptist in what is today Bethany-on-the-Jordan in the Kingdom of Jordan, a distance of fewer than some twelve miles (twenty km).
3. It has been suggested that previously, the market for such lambs had been held opposite the Temple, on the Mount of Olives.

10. *Deliver Us from Evil*

1. This is why they referred to Jonathan Maccabeus and his "unqualified" successors as "the wicked priest" (*Kohein ha-Resha,* literally meaning "bad priest").
2. Whether this is the same Judas, son of Hezekiah, who had organized a rebellion ten years earlier upon the death of Herod the Great is a matter of debate. What is clear, however, is that this new Judas movement was motivated by religious principles rather than a thirst for revenge.
3. Josephus claims that the Judas movement eventually coalesced into the Zealots, who eventually precipitated the Jewish War against the Romans in 66 CE. Recent scholarship, however, has questioned whether Judas the Galilean was indeed the force behind the Zealots. For example, the later Zealot movement wholeheartedly believed in guerilla warfare and argued that the Jews should not shrink "from the slaughter" in the struggle for freedom.
4. Zias, Joe, "Health and Healing in the Land of Israel: A Paleopathological Perspective," in: *Mikhmanim,* Spring 1999.
5. Josephus, *Antiquities*, VIII.2 §5.

6. Bultmann, Rudolph, *The Gospel of John*. Westminster: John Knox Press, 1971.

7. Meier, John P., *A Marginal Jew: Rethinking the Historical Jesus, Vol. 2*. New York: Doubleday, 1994; Chapter 18.

8. In the 1990s, a researcher at the University of Southern California, Dr. Valerie Hunt, developed the so-called Bioenergy Field Monitoring System (BFMS) that measured the human energy field up to 200KHz. She posited that any interruptions in the field could be associated with illness or disease.

9. Tacitus, *Annals,* 1:80; 6:27, 32. Also Suetonius, *Tiberius,* 63.

10. Josephus, *Antiquities*, XVIII.3 §2.

11. Hirsen, James, *Roman Law and Jesus,* doctoral research essay, 2007. Santa Barbara: Fielding Graduate University.

12. Statista Research Department, Oct 10, 2022.

13. Esau McCaulley, "What Supporters of Gun Rights Mean When They Talk About Evil," in *The New York Times,* June 10, 2022. https://www.nytimes.com/2022/06/10/opinion/mass-shooting-evil.html?searchResultPosition=1, retrieved December 2, 2022.

11. Reconstructing the Passion

1. *Antiquities of the Jews*, XVIII, Chapter 3: 63. I have deliberately omitted passages in this paragraph that are most likely interpolations by later Christian copyists of Josephus' works.

2. For a complete text, see https://www.earlychristianwritings.com/text/gospelpeter-brown.html.

3. That is why full sessions of the Sanhedrin usually took place in the *Lishkat La-Gazit,* the Chamber of Hewn Stones in the Temple.

4. Philo, *Embassy to Gaius,* 302; my italics.

Epilogue: The Splintering of Christianity

1. Tertullian, *Apologeticus,* 40.

2. For a detailed description of the Worms trial, in which Luther was compelled to defend his ideas in front of King Charles V, see Jean-Pierre Isbouts, *Ten Prayers that Changed the World*. Random House, 2016.

3. Erick Eckholm, "Firm to Remove Bible References from Gun Sights," in *The New York Times,* January 21, 2010.

ABOUT THE AUTHOR

Prof. Jean-Pierre Isbouts is one of the most prominent and prolific biblical historians today. A bestselling author, he has written a number of National Geographic books on biblical history that have sold over two million copies. These include *The Biblical World* (2006), *In the Footsteps of Jesus* (2011 and 2016), *Who's Who in the Bible* (2013), and *The Story of Christianity* (2015).

Isbouts' appeal is rooted in the fact that, as a historian, he writes about Judeo-Christian traditions from a strictly non-denominational viewpoint. This has garnered him a large following across Christians of many faith traditions, both in the United States and abroad. For example, in January 2021 one of his principal platforms, The Great Courses Company, released his 24-lecture series *History and Archaeology of the Bible*, which was an instant success. This was followed in 2022 by his course series *Searching for the Historical Jesus* on the Wondrium platform.

Other books by Dr. Isbouts include *From Moses to Muhammad: The Shared Origins of Judaism, Christianity, and Islam* (Bertelsmann); *Ten Prayers that Changed the World* (Random House), which won the 2016 Best Spirituality Book Award; and *The Archaeology of the Bible* (National Geographic). In October of 2021, National Geographic released his 650-page hardcover entitled *The Ultimate Visual History of the World*.

In 2019, Dr. Isbouts announced the results of multispectral studies by two independent laboratories, showing that a copy of Leonardo da Vinci's famous *Last Supper* in a remote abbey in Belgium was actually painted by Da Vinci and his workshop. The news produced headlines around the world, and he was featured, among others, on NBC's "Today" show. The discovery also inspired a film, *The Search for the Last Supper*, starring Alessandro Demcenko as Leonardo da Vinci, which was broadcast on PBS stations and on networks throughout the world.

Dr. Jean-Pierre Isbouts is Professor Emeritus in Human Development at Fielding Graduate University in Santa Barbara, CA. He also serves as the managing editor of Fielding University Press, which he founded in 2013.